THE ETHICAL ANIMAL

by C. H. Waddington

THE UNIVERSITY OF CHICAGO PRESS

The University of Chicago Press, Chicago 60637
The University of Chicago Press, Ltd., London

© 1960 by George Allen & Unwin Ltd.
Phoenix Edition 1967. Midway Reprint 1975
Printed in the United States of America

International Standard Book Number: 0-226-86798-6
Library of Congress Catalog Card Number: 61-12788

PREFACE

THIS book is an attempt to establish a certain thesis about the nature of the framework within which our ethical beliefs should be evaluated and criticized. To summarize the argument very briefly, I shall try to support the following four points: Firstly, that the human system of social communication functions as such an efficient means of transmitting information from one generation to the next that it has become the mechanism on which human evolution mainly depends. Secondly, that this system of 'socio-genetic' transmission can operate only because the psychological development of man is such that the new born baby becomes moulded into a creature which is ready to accept transmitted information; and, I shall suggest, it is an empirically observed fact that this acceptance is founded on the formation of 'authority-bearing' systems within the mind which also result in the human individual becoming a creature which goes in for having beliefs of the particular tone that we call ethical. Thirdly, I argue that observation of the world of living things reveals a general evolutionary direction, which has a philosophical status similar to that of healthy growth, in that both are manifestations of the immanent properties of the objective world. Finally, I conclude that any particular set of ethical beliefs, which some individual man may advance, can be meaningfully judged according to their efficacy in furthering this general evolutionary direction.

This chain of arguments was first put forward, in a somewhat undeveloped form it is true, in a number of articles published in the early 'forties. They caused a good deal of discussion, some of which was brought together in a book entitled *Science and Ethics*. Many of those who discussed my remarks, either to agree or disagree with them, did not seem to me to have fully grasped what I was trying to say, doubtless owing to my failure to express it clearly. It seemed to be often assumed that I was merely repeating, in a somewhat modernized form, the old arguments for the 'evolutionary ethics' of Herbert Spencer and the Social Darwinists; and these were countered by a reference to Moore's well-known refutation of the 'Naturalistic Fallacy'. In this book I have therefore tried to deal more explicitly with the

5

criticisms of philosophers who argue either that ethics cannot be meaningfully discussed from a naturalistic point of view, or that they cannot be rationally discussed at all.

Julian Huxley[1] is the author whose opinions come nearest to those which I am putting forward. Indeed, in his *Evolution and Ethics* he states that 'Dr Waddington's challenging thesis gave me the first impetus to a radical treatment of the subject', and he expressed general agreement with many of my arguments, to which in fact his own earlier writings had greatly contributed. More recently, in his preface to Teilhard de Chardin's *The Human Phenomenon*, he has expressed the view that his attempt to relate the development of moral codes and religions to the general trends of evolution was 'inadequate'. If this is indeed the case, in my opinion the inadequacy is to be sought in a failure to realize the full intricacy of the way in which man's ethical activities are related to his evolutionary mechanism. Huxley argues, correctly enough, that our ethical beliefs have evolutionary consequences; but he does not—or at least not consistently—make the point that the functioning of our socio-genetic mechanism demands that we should accept some sort of authority, and ethical beliefs are one of the kinds that in practice play this role. The absence, or weakness, of this link in his chain of argument laid some of Huxley's statements open to attack from philosophical opponents of the alleged 'Naturalistic Fallacy'.

In this book I have attempted to develop the argument in a way which cannot be so easily misunderstood. I am very conscious that the task of exposition is a difficult one, since it is necessary to venture not only outside my own area within biology into neighbouring disciplines in which I am not expert, such as studies on animal learning and social behaviour, but even further afield into psychology, sociology, anthropology, and finally outside the boundaries of science altogether, into philosophy. I can only hope that at least some of my fumbling statements in these fields will convey not too inaccurately the thoughts

---

[1] Detailed references have, in general, not been given in the body of the text, but the works cited will be found, under the author's name, in the list at the end of the book; when there could be some doubt as to which of an author's works is in question, a footnote identifying the reference by date has been provided.

I am trying to express. If this is so, much of the credit must go to several friends who have read and criticized drafts of the manuscript, particularly Dr R. J. Spilsbury, who discussed fully with me the more philosophical chapters, and Dr Margaret Mead, who gave me much helpful advice particularly about anthropological and psychological topics.

Some of the material incorporated in Chapters 9, 10 and 15 has been taken from, respectively: a Woodhull Lecture delivered in 1959 to the Royal Institution of Great Britain; a lecture to the Conference on 'Darwin and Sociology' held in Edinburgh in 1959; and the second Ernest Jones Lecture to the British Psychoanalytical Society, given in 1947. These lectures have been published in full in the periodicals cited in the list of references under Waddington 1947, 1959b and 1960; I am grateful to the editors concerned for permission to use the material again in this book.

C. H. W.

Edinburgh

CONTENTS

THE ETHICAL
ANIMAL

CHAPTER 1

The Importance of Ethics

IN the last two centuries man has brought into being entirely new conditions for human life. Two of his age-long preoccupations—the harnessing of power and the conquest of disease—have quite suddenly passed over into a phase of enormously accelerated growth, which in effect has created a qualitatively new situation. If a Roman of the Empire could be transported some eighteen centuries forward in time he would have found himself in a society which he could without too great a difficulty have learned to comprehend. Horace would have felt himself reasonably at home as the guest of Horace Walpole, and Catullus would soon have learned his way about among the sedan chairs, the patched-up beauties and flaring torches of London streets at night. But if the time translation had lasted for another two centuries they would have found themselves in the position of bewildered children, their daily life dominated by the automobile, the telephone, the inexorable time-table of relationships with innumerable people who form inescapable links in ever-ramifying chains of administrative arrangements without which the simplest necessities of life, a draught of water (from a municipally-owned water supply), a visit to a friend (on a public bus service), the reading of a book (from a public library) cannot be carried on. For the common man, who had no privileged position but earned his living by his own labour, the change would have been even greater. The rural peasant or blacksmith of Roman times would find his modern counterpart, the urban industrial or clerical worker, as strange as a being of a different species.

The recent metamorphosis in the human condition has been extraordinarily rapid. Four lifetimes at most could cover the essential transition. Man's adaptability is so great that we often fail to realize the magnitude of this change, which is so near to us that we can almost remember it as part of our own experience. From a more distant and future viewpoint, the discovery which Whitehead called 'the invention of the method of invention', and the revolutionary consequences of the first century or so of its application, will probably seem to have produced changes in the human condition comparable only to those brought about by the invention of urban community life in the Neolithic period.

Like the invention of urban civilization, the modern discoveries have been made and applied in relatively restricted parts of the world. They originated in western Europe, and spread from there very rapidly to the European-dominated parts of the world, such as North America and Australia. One of the most striking features of the technological advance has been an increase in speed of communication and transportation. It is therefore an essential and inescapable feature of the whole situation that it should spread with great rapidity over the world as a whole. The property of being indifferent to mere geographical distance, or complete master of it, is as much an intrinsic property of the new knowledge as fluidity is an intrinsic property of water. Once technological advance had reached a certain level in the regions of its origin, it was bound to sweep over the rest of the world like the flood waters of a river which has burst its banks. We saw it reach a few countries such as Russia and Japan in the early years of this century. In the few decades that remain before the century closes, it is inevitable that the fertilizing flood will cover the whole of the rest of the world's surface, as the waters of the Nile spread over the parched soil of the Egyptian valley.

It has been difficult to describe this process without implying, as was done in the last sentence at least, that it is 'a good thing', and that the recent changes in the human condition can be considered as progress. In western Europe, where the whole process originated and has been going on longest, the word progress is now extremely unfashionable. Anyone who is bold enough to assert that it has occurred, or even that the word has a definite meaning, is likely to be dismissed as merely naive and unsophisticated. I hope to show that this accusation is unjustified. One can be quite sophisticated—I think quite sophisticated enough—and still believe in progress. At any rate, it must be recognized that the conventional response of modern western intellectuals to the idea of progress is an exceedingly provincial one. The hundreds of millions of people living in India and China have still an expectation of life at birth which is only about half of that of the western European. The major political force which is shaping man's history in our time is the conviction of these people that to die at eighty after a healthy life using inanimate sources of power is, in some real and undeniable sense, better than to die at forty after a life of back-breaking labour, hunger and sickness. It is, in my opinion, merely a confession of intellectual inadequacy if the western intellectual finds himself forced to confess that he cannot see any way in which this belief can be rationally justified. Yet that is the position in which the official philosophy, of Great Britain at least, seems to be. The scientists and technologists who are actively engaged in the enormously complex co-operative effort by which the human condition is being changed usually find less difficulty in agreeing that the scientific revolution has value, but few have attempted to give a rational exposition of what the concept of value may mean and how values may be judged. This is what I shall try to do in this book.

The writing of these essays was provoked not only by the technological advance in the situation of human life but by another aspect of twentieth-century existence which again presents an inescapable challenge to the philosophical theory of ethics. In the 'thirties we were brought face to face with the massive existence of evil as a major factor in human affairs. Human destructiveness and the desire to massacre one's enemies are, of course, commonplaces of history. However, the Nazi's use of scientific technology to carry out a policy of racial genocide, and the sophisticated utilization by new social movements, such as Nazism, Fascism and Communism, of torture and systematic falsehood as orthodox methods of political action, forced on nearly the whole world a profound reconsideration of the problem of ends and means.

Since then the problem of destructiveness has become even more urgent. The development of the A-bomb, its use at Hiroshima and Nagasaki, and the later development of the even more devastating H-bomb, have forced mankind to realize that enormously destructive acts are technically very easily possible. It might seem that the very magnitude of these effects is such that the ethical problem largely solves itself. It needs, one might think, no elaborate intellectual apparatus to persuade any sensible person that the H-bomb is a bad thing. But that is in fact by no means the end of the matter. Life so often consists of a choice between evils. It may require quite subtle thought to enable us to decide whether the use of an H-bomb is more or less evil than some other course of action open to us. Quite recently, for instance, in the summer of 1958, the newspapers have told us that the President of the United States was almost unable to conceive that any one of his countrymen could consider the possibility that it might be better to surrender to Russia than to carry out a full-scale atomic war with her. In the face of such an opinion one can hardly maintain that the recognition of the evil of atomic weapons is unqualified.

In the essays which I wrote in the 'forties I was concerned mainly to discover what rational grounds could be found for rejecting the creeds which prescribed racial superiority and the complete subordination of means to ends. I made little attempt to deal with the cognate problem, which now appears to me of almost equal importance: the problem, namely, of why man has so often embraced systems which one might have thought he would have intuitively recognized to be evil. I shall discuss this problem rather more fully in Chapter 13.

The development of the atomic bomb has also dramatized another type of question, which has become a very actual one for ethical theory in this century. As is well known, the explosion of atomic weapons produces ionizing radiations which eventually become widespread over the whole earth. These radiations produce harmful effects, such as the development of cancers or the induction of harmful hereditary mutations. Something of an intellectual problem is posed by the fact that we cannot tell in which individuals these effects will be induced. The ethical problem can no longer be phrased in terms of personal relationships. The decision to explode the bombs, probably in a programme of weapon testing, has been taken by a super-personal machinery of government, and it may be quite impossible to indict any one

16

individual as ultimately responsible. Even if such a person could be named, the harmful effects will occur in individuals whom he will certainly never meet, and who can in fact never be certainly identified. The gene mutations and cancers consequent on bomb fall-out all occur as an addition to an unavoidable background of such calamities, which are part of the natural heritage of man.

Just how should we judge them ethically? Is it as evil for a state to order the explosion of a bomb, whose fall-out will ulti-mately, over several generations, cause the death of, say, a thousand people from harmful gene mutations, as it is for another state to order its police to shoot a thousand people personally in the back of the head? I do not think the answer is altogether obvious. Again, if ionizing radiation causes harmful gene muta-tions and cancers, it will do so equally if it is derived from what we consider natural sources instead of from human technical devices. The fall-out from bombs exploded in weapon testing up to date is estimated to have produced about a hundredth of the natural background radiation which a person is bound to accumu-late over a period of thirty years. It is, then, equivalent to the dose of radiation which he will receive every four months of his life. If the average age at which the people in a population re-produce were to advance by as little as four months, this would therefore have the same hereditary effect on future generations as the programme of weapon testing. (Such an advance in the age of reproduction would not necessarily have the same effect on the induction of cancer as the weapon testing, which has brought into being a very potent and unnatural substance— strontium 90.) What then are we to conclude, either as to the responsibility of the individual to have children as early as pos-sible and thus to run less risk of passing on mutated genes to his offspring, or of governments actually to encourage early mar-riage and reproduction?

The results of testing atomic weapons faces us with the most pressing example of a very general question which may be called the problem of the ethics of stochastic processes. We are learn-ing now to understand many situations in which some action which we may take will influence the frequency of occurrence of some phenomenon without simultaneously determining the exact

17

instance in which the effect will occur. If we increase the consumption of cigarettes there is every reason to believe that the incidence of lung cancer will rise, but we cannot say that John Smith of such-and-such an address will be killed by the disease. If we as a society put another million cars on to the road, or even if we ordain a new Bank Holiday to enable people to enjoy themselves over a long weekend in summer, we can calculate fairly precisely how many people will be killed as a direct consequence.[1]

What is the ethical status of acts of this kind? The old utilitarian cliché, which related good to the greatest happiness of the greatest number, was never very perspicuous and it becomes no easier to see one's way through the problems it poses now that the development of more refined statistical methods enables us to penetrate much further into the remote consequences of what might at first sight seem relatively neutral activities. But the problem is one of the most fundamental importance. The ends which, as his social activities convince us, twentieth-century man in the world as a whole finds overwhelmingly good are in the main attributes of stochastic processes. The most powerful forces operating in the world with which we have to grapple, intellectually and morally, are directed towards ends such as changes in the statistical indices of infant mortality or nutrition. For mankind as a whole in our time, the subtle modalities of inter-personal relationships are not the kernel of the matter. The idea of the good, as we see it forcing the pace of historical change around us, is not by any means only, or even most importantly, concerned with inter-individual reactions. It can hardly be expressed except in terms of statistical parameters.

The theory of ethics is, of course, a part of philosophy, and possibly many people will maintain that, in introducing an ethical discussion by the kind of considerations which have been mentioned in this chapter, I have merely betrayed a bias which must vitiate everything which comes later. I have shown, they might claim, that I shall merely be arguing a case which has been

[1] These sentences were written in New York City at about the time of the Labour Day holiday in 1958. The newspapers printed an estimate made, I think, by the City Transport Authorities that there would be 420 fatal automobile accidents during the holiday weekend. A few days later when the actual figures were available it was found that there had, in fact, been 418.

decided on other grounds before the intellectual argumentation starts. I should counter this charge by claiming that it stems from a misunderstanding of the relationship between the intellect and the surrounding circumstances of life. A philosopher cannot be, and I think should not aim at being, divorced from the conditions of human existence in the world of his time.

The human intellect is an instrument which has been produced during the course of evolution, primarily by the agency of natural selection, supplemented by the specifically human evolutionary processes which we shall discuss later. Like all other products of evolution, it has been moulded by the necessity to fit in with—or rather, to put it more actively, to cope with—the rest of the natural world. Its function is not to produce a God-like vision of the human situation seen from some stand-point above and outside the turmoil of actual life. The intellect is an instrument forged—perhaps by a rather rough and ready village blacksmith, let us confess—for the specific purpose of coming to terms with things. The situation with which we find ourselves confronted, a world of social-economic revolutions, of wars, of mass scale technology, is the basic raw material by which the intellect is challenged. To discuss subjects such as ethical theory without specific reference to such problems is to run away to an ivory tower.

Of course, the temptation to do this is very real, since the intellect is not really like the kind of tool which can be produced by a village blacksmith. Its overwhelming importance is just that it is an instrument for going beyond the immediate present. It is misused, or under-used, if it is only employed to provide a verbal justification for some conclusion which has been previously arrived at by non-intellectual means. This is the other pole of the situation, which one has to balance against the equally relevant fact that the intellect also remains under-used if it does not grapple with the major problems which its milieu offers. What is demanded of each generation is a theory of ethics which is neither a mere rationalization of prejudices, nor a philosophical discourse so abstract as to be irrelevant to the practical problems with which mankind is faced at that time.

One does not demand, of course, that an ethical theory should propound solutions to all the problems of its day. Theories, whether philosophic or scientific, are normally put forward by people who have an interest in the processes of thought. It is only rarely that the same individuals are equally at home in the practical world of politics, administration or experiment. What is demanded of an ethical theory is primarily that it should be relevant, and applicable to a world in which the crucial actions of a thousand million people are predicated on the belief that scientific technology is good. The intellect will have failed to carry out the functions for which evolution designed it if it issues merely in the conclusion that it can suggest no criteria by which one could hope to decide whether this belief has either meaning or validity. We must cudgel our brains to be able to do better than that. In forcing our reason to face the circumstances of its time, we need not of course place it in the position of becoming a mere servant of the situation. We must be prepared to find that a thousand million people might be wrong; but it is perhaps legitimate to feel that we should need extremely strong reasons for coming to such a conclusion. One should anticipate that, at least as a first step, we could discover some way of formulating the situation in rational terms which would allow that this great mass of the human population was talking some variety of sense, and had at any rate a great deal of justification for what it said. A priori one would expect that it would only be as a second step, if at all, that one could pass beyond this to show in what way the conclusion which they had arrived at was inadequate and could be improved on. Official philosophy, which so cleverly denies even meaning to the most powerful human convictions, is perhaps too ready to believe that it is several steps in advance of an understanding which the more sceptical may doubt whether it has ever attained.

One of the main arguments of this book is that philosophers have for the most part concerned themselves with an issue which is actually not the most important one which the ordinary man would wish to see debated. What we, as people with our lives to carry on, are seeking is some guidance by which we can direct our activities. By the time we begin to reflect rationally about such matters we find ourselves provided with a set of feelings of right and wrong, of obligation, of beliefs that we ought to do so and so and ought not to do something else. Many of these feelings have a common quality which we acknowledge by grouping them together under the common name 'ethical'. They present themselves to us as guides to action. Philosophers have in general felt that their task was, in the first place, to clarify the nature of these ethical feelings; and some have gone further and tried to distil from them general principles which would both be guides to action and would still remain ethical in quality. I shall argue that the most sensible and convincing guides to action do not necessarily possess in their own right the ethical quality, though they may come to acquire it after they have been fully accepted as applicable to our behaviour.

We have learnt that systems of feeling to which it is difficult to deny the title of ethical may lead to actions which it is equally difficult to refrain from qualifying as evil; as, for instance, the mass murder of Jews by the Nazis, or some aspects of the subjection of means to ends by the Soviet and Chinese Communists. Again, in the field of the stochastic phenomena referred to earlier, human actions have consequences of a kind which seem to demand that the actions be the subject of ethical feelings, and yet we may find those feelings absent, unduly weak or contradictory. These and some other points bring us to the realization that what we are really looking for is a criterion which will enable us to criticize, modify and expand the ethical systems with which we find ourselves unreflectively provided. Now a criterion for judging an ethical system need not be, indeed perhaps it cannot be, itself an ethical system in the ordinary sense. One could perhaps use the word 'ethical' with a small 'e' to refer, as it does at present, to the feelings and beliefs in which we recognize that quality, and use the word 'Ethical' with a capital 'E' for the criterion which we must seek to develop, which would enable us to form rational judgments about the ethical with a little 'e'. I think, however, that it is preferable to use a quite different word for the criterion, one which does not imply that it automatically shares in the particular quality which we recognize as ethical, and yet one which has a quality which we do not find it too difficult to acknowledge as good. Perhaps the word 'wisdom' is the most suitable that can be suggested.

In the essay which was written in the early 'forties, the distinction between ethics and Ethics, or between ethics and wisdom, was not explicitly recognized, although it is clearly implied in the whole course of the argument. It is particularly in connection with the philosophical criticisms of 'evolutionary ethics' that the distinction becomes most important, and it is more fully discussed in Chapter 5.

Wisdom—like the notion of the good, which in my opinion it should replace as the goal of rational endeavour—remains for mortal man an aspiration and not an achievement. Let no one be under the illusion that this book pretends to offer it in potted and easily assimilable form. The best that can be attempted is to indicate the general area in which it is to be sought, and perhaps some of the ways in which it may be approached.

CHAPTER 2

Human Value and Biological Wisdom

IT is the thesis of this book that the framework within which one can carry on a rational discussion of different systems of ethics, and make comparisons of their various merits and demerits, is to be found in a consideration of animal and human evolution. Discussions in which the notions of evolution and ethics are brought together are frequently referred to by the general title 'evolutionary ethics'. It should be recognized that this is a portmanteau term covering a number of different varieties of theory. At the end of the. last century Herbert Spencer and others advanced theories of a 'Social Darwinist' kind, involving such notions as the inevitablity of progress and the application of such slogans as the survival of the fittest or the struggle for existence to human social affairs. These theories have been so completely discredited that at this time little further needs to be said about them.[1]

The more recent phase of evolutionary ethical thought beginning in the early 1940s also comprises a number of rather different methods of approach. At one extreme we have discussions framed in terms of extremely wide scope, which treat of evolution not only in the animal world but throughout the cosmos, and attempt to relate such broad concepts to man's religious and spiritual life. The pre-eminent example of this tendency in recent years is Teilhard de Chardin, but a rather similar approach can be found in the works of several biologists, such as Conklin, Holmes and Huxley. The opposite tendency, which of course is also found expressed to various extents in these authors, particularly in Julian Huxley, is the attempt to demonstrate, in a logically coherent argument, a real connection between evolutionary processes and man's ethical feelings. The present work

[1] Cf. Waddington, 1941a; Hofstadter, 1955.

belongs definitely towards this end of the spectrum covered by the phrase 'evolutionary ethics' as did my earlier writings on the subject. Although the points I shall be making are certainly not without importance from a religious point of view, or viewed as factors in man's spiritual life, I shall not attempt to treat them in this manner, nor to venture into the field of inspirational writing of which Teilhard de Chardin and Huxley have provided us with such splendid examples. My purpose is rather the more pedestrian one of attending to the plumbing—attempting to forge somewhat stronger links in the chain of argument by which evolution and ethics are, it is suggested, connected with one another.

Another biologist whose writings on this topic have been primarily devoted to laying the logical foundations for a theory of evolutionary ethics is Chauncey D. Leake. His article 'Ethicogenesis' was published quite shortly after my *Science and Ethics* and like it led to a discussion between a scientist and a philosopher, the latter role being taken in this place by Professor Patrick Romanell.

Although I am in agreement with many of the conclusions to which Leake comes, the steps by which he gets there are, in my opinion, not really satisfactory. Leake attempts to formulate 'a naturally operative principle that governs human conduct' and arrives at the following tentative statement: 'The probability of survival of a relationship between individual humans, or groups of humans, increases with the extent to which that relationship is mutually satisfying.' It is implied that the concept of 'good' develops in a manner which is dependent upon these more or less satisfying behaviour patterns.

Now, in the first place this appears to me to be formulated in too general a manner. The statement would apparently apply, for instance, to economic arrangements between human groups. There is nothing in it which acknowledges the special character of certain types of rules of behaviour which we recognize by calling them ethical. Again, the concept of satisfaction clearly needs clarification. The statement would, for instance, clearly be inadequate unless one could guard against interpreting satisfying to mean 'ethically or morally satisfying'; but if it does not mean ethically satisfying is it clear that the application of the principle would explain the existence of behaviour codes which are based on ethical value? Finally, is the principle as stated even true? Is it clear that the relationships that are satisfying, in some sense of this word, are not in danger of being superseded by other relationships that may be more efficient in terms of the processes by which human evolution is carried on?

I shall not discuss further Leake's attempt to formulate a logical relation between ethics and evolution but shall proceed to explain my own thesis in this connection. It will perhaps be best to begin by summarizing these arguments before discussing them in more detail in later chapters.[1]

I should like to begin by accepting the fact that we know, in a rough way at least, what we are talking about when we discuss ethics. For every human being there are some propositions which he considers to be ethical, that is to say, to relate to goodness and badness or duty and obligation. The quality by virtue of which we name these propositions as ethical is recognized as such, and is not identical with any other quality such as pleasurableness, desirability, etc. I shall not be directly concerned with the question of whether goodness or obligation is the more fundamental category of ethical feeling.

Most discussions of ethics start by attempting to define goodness in terms of other concepts, such as, for instance, those just mentioned. The present argument starts in quite a different way by considering the developmental processes which lead to the formation of the concept of the good.

In this argument we shall be concerned with three related meanings of 'ethics'. It will be as well to begin distinguishing them at this point. When we speak of ethical beliefs we usually have in mind such notions as the wickedness of murder or lying, the goodness of loving kindness or truthfulness, and the like.

---

[1] This summary follows in general the pattern of a synopsis of the argument which was printed at the end of my book on *Science and Ethics* (pp. 134–6) and which also appeared at the beginning of the Symposium published by the Aristotelian Society. However, should any reader be interested enought to compare that earlier summary with the present one he will discover that in the intervening period the argument has been developed and I hope strengthened in a number of different ways, although not altered in essentials.

These are explicit ethical beliefs which gradually become formulated and accepted or rejected from the time of, say, middle childhood onwards for a varying period into our more adult life. It is to them that the phrase 'ethical belief', when used without other qualification, can most appropriately be applied. We shall be concerned, however, with types of mental activity related to ethics which go on both at earlier and at later periods in human development. The human infant is born with probably a certain innate capacity to acquire ethical beliefs but without any specific beliefs in particular. During the first few months of life processes go on by which these innate potentialities become realized. The infant becomes moulded into the sort of being who, we may say, 'goes in for' having ethical beliefs. It becomes what one might call an 'ethics participant' or an 'ethicizing' being. The process of turning the newborn infant into an ethicizing being is what I previously referred to by such phrases as 'the formation of the concept of the good'. It is a process which can, and I think should, be thought about in abstraction from any consideration of what particular ethical system is adopted, or what special notion of the good is acquired. Turning towards the other end of individual development, we shall have to consider processes in which a man examines his own ethical beliefs in relation to general systems of thought—for instance, philosophical or scientific thought—which may themselves carry little or none of the specific quality to which the name ethical is given. In so far as he then accepts some and rejects other ethical beliefs, he will be applying what might be called a supra-ethical criterion. This, which I referred to earlier as 'the general good' or 'the ethical system of general validity' is the type of criterion which in the previous chapter I referred to as 'wisdom'.[1]

[1] 'Ethical' and 'moral'. For most purposes these two words can be considered as equivalent and interchangeable. In order not to suggest a distinction which I am not particularly concerned to make, I normally use only one of them, namely 'ethical'. This has, perhaps, a rather more general meaning than 'moral', which tends to contain some reference to the morals of a particular culture in which an individual happens to be reared, and is therefore not so appropriate either in connection with the early phase of development into an ethicizing being (which must happen in a roughly similar manner in all cultures) or to the latest phase in which a man may apply a rational criterion to his ethical beliefs and thus to some extent transcend his cultural milieu. In the intermediate phase, during which a person

In the lifetime of any human individual these three types of activity—becoming an ethicizing being, formulating one particular system of ethical beliefs, and criticizing those beliefs by some supra-ethical criterion of wisdom—are not clearly separated in time but certainly overlap with one another. At the same time as a child becomes ethicizing it acquires certain definite ethical beliefs; and as it goes on formulating these beliefs in a more and more definite and specific way, it becomes more fully the sort of being that goes in for having ethical feelings. Similarly, at a later stage in life, rationally formulated criteria for criticizing ethical systems soon acquire an ethical value of their own in the mental make-up of the person who holds them. But this overlap in time should not prevent us recognizing that the three processes are in important ways different in kind.

We now believe that normal introspection reveals only rather little of the mental processes which have actually been operative in the first two of these developments. This is, of course, quite obvious in relation to our conversion into ethicizing beings, about which we in general remember remarkably little. Psychoanalysts in particular have pointed out that it is also true in connection with the better verbalized ethical notions which we acquire 'at our mother's knee'. In both these early phases, unconscious mental processes play an enormously important role, and they appear to be of a much more peculiar and unexpected nature than might have been guessed. However, it is important to note that they essentially involve interaction between the person under consideration and his external environment, in particular, other people. The most important point for our argument is the contention that the moulding of the newborn infant into an ethicizing being is not due wholly to intrinsic forces, but requires an interaction between him and his external circumstances. The adoption of this step in the argument involves the

acquires his main stock of formulated ethical beliefs, these can quite properly be referred to as moral beliefs, since they are, to an overwhelming extent, determined by the particular culture in which he is being reared. However, even if they may be culturally determined, moral beliefs are believed by individuals. A concept such as 'the moral beliefs of that particular culture' is a derivative abstract notion which requires cautious handling if one is not to commit Whitehead's Fallacy of Misplaced Concreteness.

acceptance of a strong naturalistic element in ethics. It should be pointed out, however, that for present-day biology the old alternative, between a naturalistic ethic arising wholly from the external world and a non-naturalistic ethic arising wholly from innate qualities of man, appears quite unsatisfactory. We no longer think in terms of such a black and white either-or. No characteristic of a living thing arises either wholly from nature or wholly from nurture. We are always dealing with systems which have certain innate potentialities which are realized to a greater or lesser extent, or in different forms, according to the external circumstances in which they find themselves.

The next step in the argument depends on a consideration of the mechanism of human evolution. Individuals of the species *Homo sapiens* have, of course, the same general biological make-up as other animals. Like their sub-human relatives, they pass on genetical information through their gametes from one generation to the next, and this provides the raw materials with which natural selection brings about Darwinian evolution. But on top of, and in addition to, this biological mechanism of hereditary transmission, man has developed another system of passing information from one generation to its followers. This is the process of social teaching and learning, and it constitutes in effect a secondary mechanism by which evolution can be brought about —a mechanism of a kind which I refer to as socio-genetic.

This human system of socio-genetic transmission of information from one generation to the next can, like any other system of passing on information, only operate successfully if the information is not only transmitted but is also received. The new-born infant, in fact, has to be moulded into an information acceptor. It has to be ready to believe (in some general sense of that word) what it is told. We really require, in this context, a word related to the normal use of 'belief' in the same way that 'ethicizing' is related to the normal use of 'ethics'. A human being has to be brought into a condition where he is an 'entertainer of beliefs', someone who 'goes in for believing'. Unless this happens the mechanism of information transfer cannot operate. Once it has happened and the mechanism becomes functional then the socio-genetic system carries out a function analogous to that by which the formation and union of gametes transmits genetic information. And just as the content of hereditary transmission becomes modified by natural selection, so the content of socio-genetic transmission can be modified by analogous processes, such as the confrontation of beliefs with empirical evidence and so on.

Perhaps the most crucial step in the whole chain of argument is the thesis that the development of a newborn infant into an authority acceptor—an entertainer of beliefs—involves the formation within his mind of some mental factors which carry authority, and that it is some aspects of these same authority-bearing systems that are responsible for his simultaneous moulding into an ethicizing creature. The evidence bearing on this point will be discussed at some length in Chapter 13. Admittedly one would like to see much more direct evidence than we now have, but it appears by no means impossible for empirical studies to be carried out related to the specific question of the relationship between the processes of converting the newborn infant into, on the one hand, an ethicizing and, on the other, a belief-entertaining type of being.

If, in the meantime, the point is at least tentatively accepted, we find ourselves confronted with a quite clear-cut relationship between the existence of ethical beliefs and the evolutionary processes in the human species. So far as man's evolution is carried on by his socio-genetic system—and in effect it is so in major part—the fact that he is an ethicizing being is an essential cogwheel in the whole machine. Adopting the usual terminology of biology, we can say that the function of ethicizing is to make possible human evolution in the socio-genetic mode. Now, once we have assigned the function to a general type of activity we have a rational criterion against which to judge any particular example of that activity. To say that something has a function is not merely to assign causal efficacy to it, but implies further that the causal network of which it is a part has as a whole some general character. A particular example of the activity can then be judged by how well it brings about the realization of that character.

It is a criterion of this kind which we can hope to apply to human ethical beliefs. We have first to try to ascertain the general character of human evolution or, indeed, of animal evolution as a whole. We have then to enquire, of any particular ethical belief which comes to our attention, how effective it is in mediating this empirically ascertained course of evolutionary change.

It is as well to consider what is implied by such a mode of approach by taking as an example some aspect of human activity which is less emotionally loaded than ethical beliefs. Consider for example the activity of eating. The human newborn infant has first to develop into the sort of creature that goes in for eating. In this development innate factors probably play a much greater role, and extrinsic factors a lesser one, than they do in the development of the infant into an ethicizing being, but this alteration in the relative importance of the two types of factors is of minor consequence in the present context. Next the child will acquire certain specific food habits, becoming accustomed to and accepting a particular diet. This is a process analogous to the development of specific formulated ethical beliefs. In order to find a basis for criticizing these food habits we have first to enquire what is the function of eating. We find that it is to make possible the growth of the body. Inspecting the growth of human beings on a wide basis we discover that it manifests a general character which we describe as health. We can then ask of any particular food habit or diet how effective it is in bringing about healthy growth. The criterion we are applying here is one of general accordance with the nature of the world as we observe it. If any individual approaches a nutritionist and says that he prefers to grow in an abnormal and unhealthy manner, the nutritionist can do no more than tell him that if he does so he will be out of step with nature. The criteria, of biological wisdom in the case of ethics, or healthy growth in the case of eating, which can be derived in this way, are immanent in nature as we find it, not superposed on it from outside. However, even if one considers that there is some overriding supernatural being from whom our ethical standards are ultimately derived, it is surely blasphemous to suppose that the nature he has created is such as to deceive us as to his true wishes. Thus, even an immanent criterion, if we have discerned it aright, would not contradict, though it might of course fall short of, a supernatural one.

It may be as well to emphasize at this point that empirically derived 'normative' concepts, such as health or the course of evolution, are usually by no means simple, but could be analysed into many constituent, though probably mutually dependent, parts. Moreover, they are 'open' concepts; we can never expect to attain finality in our knowledge of them. When we say, then, that the function of eating is to promote healthy growth, or that of going in for ethics to promote human evolution, it must be understood that 'health' and 'evolution' are being used to refer to complex and subtle states of affairs. If the definition of these words is unduly restricted, we should have to assign correspondingly more functions to the activities. In particular, I use the phrase 'human evolution' to refer to all the cultural changes which differentiate human life at the present day from that of our Stone Age ancestors. It includes spiritual and intellectual changes as well as those concerning materials and tools. Thus the promotion of human evolution is not at all a restricting notion.

In fact, if it is to be criticized, it should be on the grounds that it is too inclusive rather than for being too narrow. It might be argued that it covers so much that it becomes in practice useless. However, it is probably no more open to this criticism than any other of the attempts to formulate the framework in which ethical discussion can profitably be carried on. No general ethical principle can be useful unless it is wide enough to be relevant to very many diverse aspects of life; and that implies that it cannot be precise enough to obviate the need for debate about particular moral issues.

It will be apparent from this summary that the argument I am advancing involves a number of different scientific disciplines. It had its origin in consideration of the biological situation of man, but this led me to make positive suggestions about topics which are usually said to belong to psychology, sociology and anthropology. And I found myself, like a baby sitting in the bath water, called upon to parry the attacks of well-meaning philosophers anxious to resolve semantic puzzles by emptying me, along with a lot of other alleged rubbish, down the sink. I do not feel called

upon to make much apology for the mere act of discussing subjects which the academic profession finds it convenient to assign
to some other university department than my own. Fences, after
all, are made to be jumped over, and boundaries to be crossed.
But there are practical difficulties, which I am only too conscious
of having dealt with only very inadequately. The sheer volume
of reading-matter is now so enormous, and increases so rapidly,
that no one can hope to master fully what has been written about
his own subject, let alone about other fields of intellectual endeavour with which he is not professionally concerned. I have
tried, throughout the more detailed discussion of my argument
which follows, to stick rather closely to the points at issue, and
to take account only of those aspects of the various subjects
which are really germane to what I am trying to say. Even with
that restriction, the best one could hope to do is to give an
adequately representative sample of the points which have been
made in printed discussions. It is more than likely that I have
failed even in this; if so I apologize to any of my colleagues
whose work I have, through ignorance, failed to take into
account.

The thesis I am most anxious to convey is, however, not concerned in the first instance with criticism of previous views. It
consists rather of a number of positive arguments, and although
some of these have certainly been advanced before, the general
pattern of thought makes up a whole which is at least unusual, if
not novel. Within the last year there have been two conferences
devoted to the relations between biological evolution and the
existence of man as a social being; first, the conference on
Darwin and the Social Sciences, held at Edinburgh in April 1959,
and attended by many British social scientists, and then the much
larger Darwin Centennial Conference held at Chicago in Novem-
ber, in which many American and some European experts took
part. My attendance at these conferences showed me that the
arguments I am advancing here have at least the singularity—
whether it is a favourable or unfavourable point, I leave the
reader to determine—that no one else seems to be at present
saying quite the same thing. The Chicago conference especially
was the occasion for a general survey of the present state of

opinion about many topics which are crucial for some of the arguments I shall be advancing, and I have made considerable use of its proceedings as an authoritative summary of current thought.

The main propositions I wish to advance derive from, and perhaps still belong to, the domains of the biological and social sciences. Logically prior to their discussion is the necessity to establish the propriety of engaging in rational discussion of ethical matters at all, in the face of the criticisms which recent philosophical thought has brought against the use of language for this purpose. In the next few chapters, I shall try to rebut or evade these criticisms Those readers who are not interested in philosophical arguments, or who already feel willing to grant that the discussion of ethics may be meaningful, can if they wish skip this section and proceed direct to the more scientific approach in Chapter 8.

CHAPTER 3

Squaring the Vienna Circle

IT is very difficult for ordinary people to discover how to say anything about a subject which has been extensively discussed by philosophers, and ethics is pre-eminently a field in which professional philosophers have made hay. Systems of ethical thought, replete with technical terms, have been expounded, dissected and criticized, ever since man first learnt to write. A newcomer has scarcely opened his mouth to proffer a few comments or ideas before the experts have labelled, and dismissed, him as an adherent of one or other of the recognized schools, whose weaknesses have long been exposed. The scientist receives a haughty welcome. 'We can contemplate with a smile or a sigh,' writes Dr C. D. Broad, 'the waxing and waning of each cheap and easy solution which is propounded for our admiration as the last word of "science". We know beforehand that it will be inadequate; and that it will try to disguise its inadequacy by ignoring some of the facts, by distorting others, and by that curious inability to distinguish between ingenious fancies and demonstrated truths which seems to be the besetting weakness of the man of purely scientific training when he steps outside his laboratory. And we can amuse ourselves, if our tastes lie in that direction, by noticing which well-worn fallacy or old familiar inadequacy is characteristic of the latest gospel, and whether it is well or ill-disguised in its new dress.'

This is, perhaps, scarcely the best way to overcome the scientist's common temptation to dismiss the whole of philosophy as an adolescent indulgence in unrewarding verbiage. After all in the last few hundred years, scientists have certainly demonstrated some interesting and unexpected facts about the world, even if it is, maybe, their professional philosophical colleagues who eventually show how these may best be incorporated into the

intellectual scheme by which man attempts to arrange the phenomena by which he is surrounded into some sort of order. I should
myself be willing to admit that philosophers are—in general,
and with all the usual reservations necessary for any such sweep-
ing generalization—better at doing philosophy than scientists
are; and that they sometimes suggest ways of looking at situations which scientists may find it fruitful to explore. But those
who may think that this is to give too much weight to Broad's
strictures may find some consolation in the fact that most philosophers have now themselves come to the conclusion that they
are not really concerned with distinguishing ingenious fancies
from demonstrated truths. The latter commodity is indeed one
with which philosophers are singularly ill provided.

The major points I am trying to advance are actually scientific
hypotheses, and do not belong to the sphere of philosophy—at
least not as philosophy is understood by the most influential
modern school, the followers of the later Wittgenstein. The concern of philosophy, according to them, is the clarification of con-
fusions which may arise as to the way in which language is or
should be used. It does not aim to bring about that type of
addition to our knowledge or understanding of topic which is
achieved by the discovery of a new fact or the proposal of a new
scientific hypothesis. 'The results of philosophy,' says Wittgenstein (1953, p. 48), 'are the uncovering of one or another piece
of plain nonsense and of the bumps that the understanding has
got by running its head up against the limits of language. . . .
Philosophy may in no way interfere with the actual use of language; it can in the end only describe it. For it cannot give it any
foundation either. It leaves everything as it is. . . . And we may
not advance any kind of theory. There must not be anything
hypothetical in our considerations. We must do away with all
explanation, and description alone must take its place. . . .
If one tried to advance theses in philosophy, it would never be
possible to question them, because everyone would agree with
them.'

At first glance, it might seem that such a view reduces philosophy to triviality. 'Where does our investigation get its importance from, since it seems only to destroy everything in-

teresting, that is, all that is great and important? (As it were all the buildings, leaving behind only bits of stone and rubble.) What we are destroying is nothing but houses of cards and we are clearing up the ground of language on which they stand.' In fact, the more one reflects on it, the more the philosopher's task of describing the use of language appears one which calls for the powers of both Hercules and Sisyphus—the cleansing of an Augean stable in which the *cacoethes scribendi* is produced anew as fast as it can be tidied away.

But one cannot wait to propound hypotheses about ethical matters—and if philosophers do not consider it their task to do so, that in no way implies that others are precluded from trying their hand—until one is provided with a precise and unambiguous language in which to frame them. Such a day will probably never dawn. It is at least possible that some degree of ambiguity and confusion is a price which a language must pay for the flexibility which is necessary if any new understanding is to be expressed in it; just as the presence of harmful genetic mutations is the inescapable condition which must be tolerated by a population so long as it retains the capacity for evolutionary change. The real difficulty which faces the layman is this, to focus attention on those few points in his thought which are, perhaps, novel; and to save them from being lost sight of under a cloud of rectifications of what are likely to be quite conventionally inadequate expressions which are being used merely as a means of conveyance to carry the argument up to the crucial point where something is to be said.

The first of the two points I want to make is the apparently simple one, that it is possible to say something meaningful about ethics. The most influential modern school of philosophy would, in the first flush of its enthusiasm, have denied it. About the time I went up to the university as an undergraduate, two works which I consider to be major poems were published. One was Eliot's 'Waste Land', the other Wittgenstein's 'Tractatus Logico-philosophicus', which was cast in the form, even more surprising than that chosen by Eliot, of a philosophical treatise—but is, I believe, essentially a poem. Around the 'Tractatus', which was originally written in German, in Vienna, there grew up a group of undoubted, professional philosophers—Carnap, Schlick and others. They formed the so-called Vienna Circle, the Wiener Kreis. And they propounded the philosophical doctrine known as Logical Positivism. It was a fine rip-roaring creed, which made a great appeal to the undergraduate mind. Putting it very crudely, its central points were, firstly, that what philosophers deal with are not facts but groups of words; and secondly, that the meaning of a group of words, if any, is nothing more than the way you would verify the proposition which the words state.

Now, of course, a great many sets of words do not state anything that can be verified, or at least it is not clear just how one would set about verifying it. And the Logical Positivists went on unhesitatingly to say that such sets of words were strictly meaningless—without sense—to the philosopher or rational man, no more than an agitation of the air, whatever they might be to the poet. Of course, Hume had said it already, a long time earlier. But the Vienna Circle not only said it again; they dressed it up in extremely elegant mathematical symbols, and they used it with effect to prick a certain number of bubbles of stale hot air. Undergraduates keeping up with intellectual fashion accepted it readily, professional philosophers more slowly but with longer lasting results; while few noticed that Wittgenstein, the original centre, was now quietly some way well outside the circumference. He admitted the possibility that some things, although inexpressible in propositions, might be 'shown', and thus he pointed to a realm of the mystical, whose importance is not diminished by the fact that we cannot discuss it. Moreover, as Russell slyly pointed out in his introduction to the 'Tractatus', Wittgenstein contrives to communicate an account of his ethical beliefs which is surprisingly explicit if we accept his view that ethics cannot be meaningfully discussed.

One of the major points made by the Logical Positivists was that statements dealing with value, such as 'Killing is evil', do not in fact assert anything which is conceivably capable of verification. According to Carnap, 'a value statement is nothing else than a command in a misleading grammatical form. . . . It does not assert anything and can neither be proved nor disproved'. They have, he says, 'no theoretical sense'. This is a conclusion which finds adherents, for instance, Professor Ayer, even thirty years later. But in the meantime, the novelty, and a good deal of the initial self-confidence, have worn off. It is a singularly un-biological point of view, which would be rejected, for instance, by elephants; as Rensch[1] has shown, these beasts can learn to attach significance to some twenty or so human words, used as commands. And one of the main arguments I am advancing is that the primitive mechanism on which the transmission of even factual statements depends must have its basis in the coupling of the statement with some element of authority. At the time it begins to operate in any newborn individual, the human system of information-transfer works independently of verification, which is a second-order process analogous to natural selection rather than to any part of the process of heredity.

Even if we do not look aside from the field of adult human communication to which Logical Positivists usually confine their attention, is verification after all such a clear-cut notion? One cannot decide whether a statement is verifiable or not until one knows what sort of procedure would constitute verifying it; that is, until one knows what it means.[2] And even if one does know how to set about verifying, the whole history of the gradual growth of scientific knowledge shows that one has never finished the task (except for 'protocol statements', which describe one's own contemporaneous observations). Anyone who wishes to see the difficulties of the 'principle of verification' should look at the Introduction which Professor Ayer wrote in 1946 to the second edition of his book, Language, Truth and Logic, the somewhat belated battle-cry on behalf of Logical Positivism which he had first published ten years earlier. Finally, it has been recognized that, even if we assume that we know what verification consists of, there is no reason to conclude that the verifiable content of a sentence necessarily exhausts its significance. In particular, in our present context, commands, although non-verifiable, are certainly items of verbal communication, and therefore have

[1] B. Rensch, 'The Intelligence of Elephants', *Sci. Amer.*, February 1957.

[2] 'Asking whether and how a proposition can be verified is only a particular way of asking "How do you mean?".' Wittgenstein, *Philosophical Investigations*, p. 112.

significance. We do not remove ethics from the realm of subjects worthy of discussion even if we conclude that the basic elements of it are commands.

In fact, Logical Positivism as it existed in the 'twenties and 'thirties is to all intents and purposes defunct. Its place has been taken by what is usually called 'Linguistic Philosophy', which differs, in the main, by recognizing that words may have meanings of many different kinds. Again it is, perhaps, Wittgenstein who has expressed most clearly the nature of this type of philosophical thought.[1] 'A philosophical problem,' he says, 'has the form: I don't know my way about. . . . Philosophy simply puts everything before us, and neither explains nor deduces anything. . . . Philosophy may in no way interfere with the actual use of language; it can in the end only describe it. For it cannot give it any foundation either. It leaves everything as it is.'

In practice this means that linguistic philosophers accept it as axiomatic that a phrase which is common usage must be meaningful, and is in some sense 'all right'. To take a recent example, W. F. R. Hardie, in an article on the old problem of free-will and determinism, begins with the question whether determinists are asking whether anyone ever acts of his own free-will. 'If so,' he says, 'the question asked was absurd. For from the fact that "of his own free will" has a standard use, and therefore an application, it follows that it is trivial to assert, and absurd to deny, that men will freely, that the will is free.' Equally, I suppose, from the fact that we often say 'My landlord has a heart of stone', it follows that it is absurd to deny that human hearts can be made of stone. Of course in a certain, but extremely complicated sense, this is true enough. But if one starts a discussion of a difficult subject like free will with a remark of this kind, it takes a very long time to clear away the mess and start saying anything interesting—especially when you have decided beforehand that commonsense, whatever that is, will turn out to be right in the end. To the mildly sceptical, the whole philosophical movement comes down to the thesis that if you talk long enough about any subject you will find that you have nothing to say about it.

[1] 1953, pp. 123, 124, 126.

Ernest Gellner has described the recent history of philosophy in terms of the old rhyme:

> The centipede was happy quite until the toad began:
> Now pray which leg goes after which?
> Which wrought his mind to such a pitch,
> He lay distracted in a ditch,
> Reflecting how to run.

Originally, he said, philosophers were unworried about how they can meaningfully speak, and wandered about in happy speculation instead. Then there was a stage, corresponding to Logical Positivism, at which as it were the centipede realized that it had two legs; philosophers considered that words had meanings of two kinds only, one dependent on the possibility of factual verification and the other concerned with purely logical implications, with the way in which a word can occur in a sequence of logical steps. Then there comes the stage of linguistic philosophy, in which the centipede realizes that it has very many different legs, and philosophers realize that words may have very many meanings of different kinds.

At that stage the philosophers have held to two beliefs. Firstly, that the only acceptable method of philosophical attack is to analyse the usage of the words in which a proposition may be stated; the only 'solution' of philosophical problems is the kind of information recorded in the *Oxford English Dictionary*. And this implies the second point, that commonsense will always be found to be justified. Gellner puts their argument as follows: 'If we do begin with a careful examination of our speech habits, in relation to the relevant terms, the only thing which is allowed to count as the successful termination of such an enquiry is a set of observations about usage showing that there really was no problem at all. We use words in certain ways, that is all, and once we see just how we use them no difficulty can be left. . . . This is a philosophy which prejudges everything, by assuming in advance that there are no real problems, by allowing nothing to count as a solution other than a demonstration from the use of words that all the fuss had been about nothing.'

This is, of course, a statement from a hostile point of view,[1]

---

[1] This is further developed in Gellner's recent book, 1959.

but it is one which I think linguistic philosophers would find some difficulty in rebutting. But in my opinion the main weakness of the linguistic philosophical school is that in fact their analysis of word usage is conducted in a manner which to the biologist seems extraordinarily old-fashioned. They usually concern themselves only with the way in which words are used by the ordinary educated adult, and neglect almost entirely to consider how these language habits have been acquired. This is as though biology were still to be confined to the methods of comparative anatomy used in the eighteenth century. The *Oxford Dictionary* corresponds at best to a magnificent text-book of anatomy. The only form of order or pattern which could be found in it would be a static one, comparable to the notion of the Great Ladder of Being, or the natural classification of Linnaeus. With the development of the sciences which deal with the time-changes of organisms, the sciences of embryology and evolution, such a point of view is completely out of date in biology. The recent studies of the psychological growth of infants and children should have made it equally out of date in philosophy.

Few philosophers seem to have realized this, but one of them was certainly Wittgenstein. During one summer, 1940, I think, or 1941, he and R. H. Thouless and I used to meet one evening every week, and spend three or four hours after dinner discussing philosophy in the Roundabout Garden of Trinity, Cambridge. The subject of most of these discourses was the relation between a word and the thing it signifies. I vividly remember those twilit evenings, when Wittgenstein would jump up from the lawn on which we had been sitting and pull out of a pocket of his shabby sports coat a matchbox or some other small object. As he held it up in front of us and tried to make us realize the impervious vacuity of the gap which exists between the object in his fingers and the auditory modulation of air pressure or the black marks on white paper by which we refer to it, his main weapon of exposition was to persuade us to shed the preoccupations of the the first year of the Second World War and to feel ourselves again children whose mother was instructing us in our first words. Something of the same method—a method which explicitly recognizes the importance of a developmental analysis of language—comes over in the first four pages or so of the *Philosophical Investigations*, but it was of course incomparably more vivid when the phrases were formulated slowly and painfully by Wittgenstein himself, his face, between the incongruously student-like, tousled, curly hair and open-necked shirt, frowning and contorted with the effort to express precisely his understanding of the way in which the relation he was discussing is inexpressible. Often, indeed, his words came to a standstill, but communication continued for some time further by the means of facial and bodily gesture. Wittgenstein was, I think, so acutely aware of the otherness of other things that he never fully reconciled himself to the fact that words can have anything to do with them. I suspect that his intense concentration on the analysis and construction of languages arose largely from some profound feeling that for him at least all languages must remain almost totally inadequate for anything he felt it important to say.

One's whole assessment of the true import of the 'Wittgensteinian revolution' in philosophy—or rather, of the two revolutions, which led first to Logical Positivism and then to Linguistic Philosophy—must, I think, be profoundly affected by one's understanding of, or reaction to, those aspects of his personal position which he maintained could not be conveyed in terms of formulated logical concepts. It was in many ways the very kernel of his message which could be offered only by an unformalized process which he referred to as 'showing', and could thus be apprehended only by an intuitive faculty akin to empathy. It can be glimpsed very obscurely behind the printed words on the page but was considerably more accessible in personal contact.

No one who met him could easily doubt that Wittgenstein was a tragic figure of some magnitude. The nature of his spiritual situation will be discussed as long as that of Rimbaud or Jackson Pollock. My tentative diagnosis of it would be this: that Wittgenstein failed to realize that what he had to convey was essentially a poetic awareness of the otherness of reality; he was led, presumably by historical accidents of which I am ignorant, to enshrine his message in a logico-philosophical jargon, whose very abstractness on the one hand served to exhibit the dislocation he felt between man and his surroundings, but on the other resulted in him being taken for a philosopher—an identification by which he was at first flattered, later filled by apprehension and a sense of guilt, but still misled; so that he took seriously the fact that in the 'Tractatus' he had written a large book about philosophy which argued in meticulous detail the thesis that writing large books about this subject is a silly thing to do. The famous penultimate paragraph of the 'Tractatus': 'My propositions are elucidatory in this way: he who understands me finally recognizes them as senseless, when he has climbed out through them, on them, over them. (He must so to speak throw away the ladder, after he has climbed up on it.)' Is not this a *poetic* paradox, as undemanding of exigesis as Eliot's lines from 'Burnt Norton':

> *Footfalls echo in the memory*
> *Down the passage which we did not take*
> *Towards the door we never opened . . .?*

Consider the steps in the argument of the 'Tractatus' so carefully numbered in section 6.4:

6·4 All 'propositions are of equal value.

6·41 The sense of the world must lie outside the world. In the world everything is as it is and happens as it does happen. *In* it there is no value—and if there were it would be of no value.
If there is a value which is of value, it must lie outside all happening and being-so. For all happening and being-so is accidental.

. . . .

6·42 Hence also there cannot be any ethical propositions. Propositions cannot express anything higher.

6·421 It is clear that ethics cannot be expressed.
Ethics are transcendental.
(Ethics and aesthetics are one.)

What is this but a pure-line descendant of the Romantic Movement?—a transcendental instead of an immanent Wordsworthianism? a statement to which logical algebra is finally no more relevant than it is to *Anna Livia Plurabelle* or some of Picasso's perspective? This is a statement which does not belong with Frege and *Principia Mathematica*, but again one is reminded of his contemporary Eliot, in 'East Coker':

> *To arrive where you are, to get from where you are not,*
> *You must go by a way wherein there is no ecstasy.*
> *In order to arrive at what you do not know*
> *You must go by a way which is the way of ignorance.*
> . . . .
> *And what you do not know is the only thing you know*
> *And what you own is what you do not own*
> *And where you are is where you are not.*

But Wittgenstein himself fell into the trap which his unlikely vocabulary so successfully spread before the feet of the pedestrian academics. Faced with the apparently unavoidable task of expounding what he had claimed to be unexpoundable—or, putting it in bread-and-butter terms, guilty as he felt himself to be of accepting a salary for teaching 'philosophy' which, on his own showing, could not or should not be taught—he took himself literally enough to fritter away the latter half of his life in persuading students not to come to his lectures, or, if they insisted, at least not to try to remember what he had said; a truly tragic nihilism of the ego, but of an ego so powerful and impressive that those who glimpsed it insisted on some record, which was forced out of him as the unfinished 'Philosophical Investigations' and the pirated 'Brown and Blue Books'. The vital Wittgenstein was anaesthetized by academic acclaim, which persuaded him that he ought to see himself as a philosopher; and he took his odd revenge by luring the academics into a desert of language-games and philosophy-as-grammatical-therapeutics, and then himself de-materializing like a will o' the wisp.

Logical Positivism in its messianic early days denied the possibility of rational discussion of ethics. One could, I think, have persuaded its devotees that some of the arguments in this book rightly belong to science, and are meaningful, but much of it would probably have been dismissed as without sense. But its own inherent inadequacies have led to the development of Logical Positivism into the Linguistic Philosophy derived from the late rather than the early Wittgenstein, and this, as the catch-phrase has it, 'leaves everything as it is'. It does not deny the possibility of discussing ethics in a way that has meaning. In fact it is difficult to discover that it has anything to contribute to the subject, except to give a renewed emphasis to the oldest platitude in all discussions—admittedly one of the most difficult to live up to satisfactorily—that one should be very careful in the use of language.

CHAPTER 4

The Relevance of Developmental Facts

UNFORTUNATELY, the interest which Wittgenstein showed in the genesis of meaning has not been widely shared by other recent philosophers. Quite often indeed such an interest is expolicitly ruled out of court and is stigmatized as 'the genetic fallacy'. Admittedly, of course, it is a mistake to suppose that if one has shown that *A* is derived from *a*, then *A* is 'nothing but' *a*. But this is so elementary that few biologists are likely to need philosophers to remind them against it. It was after all not Huxley, but Wilberforce, who was tempted to conclude that a demonstration that man was evolutionarily derived from the monkey implied that man was no more than a monkey. Scientists are certainly sufficiently aware of the dangers of such arguments to be on their guard against them, although they of course may still be advanced from time to time by inadvertence. But scientists know also that the true nature of, for instance, an Ascidian would be almost impossible to guess if one did not examine its embryonic stages and investigate its genesis. It is very difficult indeed to believe that similar types of thought would fail to be valuable if applied to the analysis of linguistic usage.

Any investigation of the development of meaning during the life history of an individual involves the ascertainment of facts. Present-day philosophers commonly maintain that there is a logical problem which is quite independent of, and dissociated from, the factual one. It is the logical problem with which they wish to concern themselves, and they feel ready to hand over all questions of fact to the natural sciences and to wash their hands of it.

For instance, Nowell-Smith writes (p. 219): 'The fundamental mistake is that of confusing three distinct sorts of questions, logical, factual and moral. The logical questions are those about the meanings of the words used in moral discourse and about the relations between moral concepts. For example, 'Can "right" be defined in terms of "good" or "fulfilment of purpose" or is it an irreducible concept?' The factual questions are mainly historical, sociological and psychological. For example, 'What rules do we actually have?', 'How did we come to adopt just this set of rules?', 'What do men, in fact, desire, enjoy, find pleasant, etc.?' And the moral questions are 'What ought I to do?', 'What rule is it best for me to adopt?'

Now the three types of questions of which Nowell-Smith provides examples are indeed different in kind; and thus far his remarks are justified. But he makes a clear distinction between logical and factual questions only by omitting to consider the kind of factual question which is relevant to his logical problems. His factual queries are concerned only with the reasons why we have certain ethical beliefs or feelings rather than others. He does not ask the question which is important in connection with logical analysis, that is, how we come to develop any ethical concepts at all; or, as I have put it, how do we become ethicizing beings? Admittedly it is not very relevant to the *logical* structure of the word 'good' to discover whether the speaker belongs to a society which approves of slavery or infanticide. But it is extremely relevant to discover, if possible, whether the experiences with which the child first associates ethical feelings are ones of simple recognition (like those involved in learning the use of the word 'red') or whether, for instance, they involve comparisons (cf. 'punctual' or 'appropriate'), or pure emotions (like 'angry'), or actions ('eating', 'playing'). If any one of these types of experience could be shown to provide the initial germ from which our later ethical beliefs grow, that could hardly fail to influence in a very important way the analysis of the logical structure of the phraseology in which the derived and elaborated moralizings of later life are conducted.

Actually, none of these examples provides a very good parallel for the manner in which ethical notions develop. As has been mentioned in a summary way in pages 26–29, the facts which give rise to notions to which we attach moral values are apprehended in a very remarkable manner, at least when the child first becomes aware of them. They seem to involve a peculiar mechanism by which external personalities become, as the psychologists say, 'introjected' into the structure of the apprehending psyche; and there may also be a further complication, in that the child may first project on to the external world certain of its own characteristics, so that when the process of introjection occurs it is, in a sense, canabalistic. These matters will be further discussed in Chapter 13. The philosophical points with which we are concerned here are two. Firstly, these problems are in theory as capable of being talked about and investigated as any other psychological questions. Admittedly, they are in fact some of the most difficult aspects of psychology to study. Admittedly, also, the criteria for judging the truth of psychological hypotheses are difficult to define, but few people nowadays would doubt that some sort of natural science of psychology is possible, and that the problem of the child's first apprehension of the notion of good and evil belongs within its domain.

The second philosophical point is that even if we were to define philosophy as the study of language, an understanding of its genesis would be as relevant and important as an analysis of current linguistic usage. There is, for instance, a well-known division of the philosophical schools into the 'teleologists', who argue that the basic ethical notion is of a kind appropriate to things, such as goodness or some equivalent concept, and an opposing group of 'deontologists', who find the foundation of ethics in ideas such as obligation, duty and the like, which apply to actions. It is surely obvious that a study of the origin of the notion of ethical value in the early years of life is more likely to lead to a solution of this problem than any analysis of the highly complex language that we have, by the time we become adult, developed for its discussions. It is equally relevant to the intuitionist theories, according to which ethical value is some quality which we merely recognize.

When the relevance of psychology to such questions is denied by philosophers—as it usually is—they normally do so on the basis of a very restricted notion as to what psychologists are interested in. For instance, Nowell-Smith writes as follows (p. 181): 'It is also true that gerundive and value judgments do not follow logically from descriptive statements about what men like, enjoy and approve of. But the reason for this is not that gerundive words and value words refer to special entities or qualities, but that the person who uses them is not, except in certain secondary cases, describing anything at all. He is not doing what psychologists do, which is to describe, explain and comment on what people like, enjoy and approve of; and he is not doing what moral philosophers do, which is to describe, explain and comment on the way in which people use moral words; he is himself using moral language, expressing approval, appraising, advising, exhorting, commending or praising.' Now, psychologists do much more than merely describe, explain and comment on what people like, enjoy and approve of. Both psychoanalysts and those using more conventional methods, such as Piaget, attempt to do nothing less than explain how it comes about that anyone should engage in the activities of expressing approval, praising, advising, exhorting, commending or appraising.

As a matter of fact, at the end of his discussion (p. 504), Nowell-Smith himself suggests a criterion drawn from the field of genetic psychology as the defining characteristic of an ethical value. 'We might therefore say,' he writes, 'that moral traits of character are just those traits that are known to be amenable to praise or blame; and this would explain why we punish idle boys but not stupid ones, thieves but not kleptomaniacs, the sane but not the insane.' But this, I think, most teachers would agree is a somewhat superficial piece of psychology. Stupidity, for instance, can certainly be influenced by praise or blame. Nowell-Smith's definition works only if by the words praise or blame he is referring to *moral* judgment; and that of course begs the question. But at least he is coming near to acknowledging that some psychological, i.e. scientific, facts or alleged facts may not be irrelevant to the questions of the meaning of ethical terms.

CHAPTER 5

The 'Naturalistic Fallacy'

ALL the discussion in the previous two chapters has been concerned with our individual notions of good and bad, and right and wrong. What does a man mean when he says that he attaches ethical value to something? Or, as the linguistic philosophers would say, in what manner are the words of ethical connotation used? These are important and interesting questions whose solution, I have argued, is to be looked for in the main in the field of psychology. But I have suggested that we would be more interested in some method of adjudicating or choosing between the different notions which come to our attention. What we want to be able to do is to discover some method of discussing, in a rational manner, whether, for example, an ethic which attaches high value to every individual life is preferable to one which condones or approves head-hunting. What I shall attempt to provide is a criterion for judging between ethical values. This criterion is not by any means the same thing as a new ethical value. We must pass on now from the discussion of ethics to Ethics; or to put it in another way, from ethics to wisdom.

It will perhaps be best to begin by a discussion of the main argument which philosophers commonly bring against any example of what is called a scientific theory of ethics. The argument is that all such theories are based on an attempt to define the good in terms of some other type of concept, such as the satisfaction of desire or pleasure and pain; such an attempt is defined as naturalism and is refuted as a fallacy. The refutation derives originally from Hume. His best known passage on the subject (from the *Treatise of Human Nature*, Book 3, Part 1, Section 1) is as follows: 'In every system of morality which I have hitherto met with, I have always remarked that the author proceeds for some time in the ordinary way of reasoning, and establishes the being of a god or makes observations concerning human affairs; when of a sudden I am surprised to find that instead of the usual copulations of propositions is and is not, I meet with no proposition that is not connected with an ought or an ought not. This change is imperceptible; but is however of the last consequence. For as this ought or ought not expresses some new relation or affirmation, it is necessary that it should be observed and explained; and at the same time that a reason should be given for what seems altogether inconceivable; how this new relation can be a deduction from others that are entirely different from it.'

This argument has been very widely adopted by modern philosophers, particularly the intuitionists who derive from G. E. Moore. Hume's thesis, that one cannot logically pass from 'is' to 'ought', reappears in the statement that it is impossible to define the good in terms of anything else; since if, for instance, we define it as 'the pleasurable', or 'the more highly evolved', one can always ask of any admittedly pleasurable or highly evolved thing whether it is also good; and this question, it is claimed, can only be answered by reference back to that very idea of the good which we were attempting to define. For instance, Sir David Ross writes, in a passage quoted by Nowell-Smith (p. 31): 'There is really no resemblance between the characteristic which we have in mind when we say "right" or "obligatory" and that which we have in mind when we say "more evolved". . . . If we ask ourselves what "more evolved" means, we shall find in it, I think, two main elements: (1) that conduct so described comes, in time, after a process of evolution of more or less duration, and (2) that it has a characteristic which usually emerges in the course of evolution, that of being complex, in comparison with the simple activities which appear in an early stage of evolution. And it is surely clear that neither temporal posteriority nor complexity, nor the union of the two, is that which we mean to refer to when we use the term "right" or "obligatory".'

The same point is put by Moore, who was one of the originators of this argument, in the following words (p. 16): 'But whoever will attentively consider with himself what is actually before his mind when he asks the question "Is pleasure (or whatever it may be) after all good?'' can satisfy himself that he is not merely wondering whether pleasure is pleasant. And if he will try this experiment with each suggested definition in succession, he may become expert enough to recognize that in every case he has before his mind a unique object. . . .'

Nowell-Smith, who quotes these passages in his book *Ethics*, proceeds to criticize the mode of expression used by Ross and Moore, which assumes that when we say that so-and-so is good, we assert that it has a certain quality in the same sense that a red object has the quality of redness. His criticisms are, I think, justified. Goodness is not the name of a quality in the same way that the words redness, hardness and so on are (though to call even the latter 'names of qualities' is perhaps not very happy). But apart from the manner of expression employed, the intuition-ists do seem to have established the point that ethical statements cannot be reduced to non-ethical statements without omitting something which they originally contained; any full translation of an ethical statement into other phrases must still include at least one ethical word.

But as Anscombe, for instance, has recently pointed out, the situation is quite similar for other non-ethical statements, such as those involving the concepts of owing or needing. 'It would be ludicrous,' she continues, 'to pretend that there can be no such thing as a transition from e.g. "is" to "owes".' But she rejects the transition from 'is' to 'ought', on the somewhat odd grounds that 'this word "ought" having become a word of mere mesmeric force could not in the character of having that force be anything whatever'. Nowell-Smith, after his verbal criticisms of the usual statements of Moore's argument, also accepts it. He does so partly on the grounds that the naturalistic argument contains logical errors (of the kind mentioned by him in the quotation given on page 49, where the inadequacy of his argument was also pointed out); and partly on the basis of a theory of his own, involving what are called pro and con attitudes, whose status in the world of fact seems to me to be left very obscure.

A very impressive list of other authoritative endorsements of the doctrine could easily be found; for instance, in the same number of *Philosophy* as that which contains Anscombe's article,

Professor Flew is quoted (p. 29) as saying: 'I think it is very important indeed to make as clear as we can, and to underline with all possible emphasis, that this is a point of inexorable logic', and this article goes on, 'Professor Popper, to take but one other example, has expressed it no less trenchantly: "Perhaps the simplest and most important point about ethics is purely logical. I mean the impossibility to derive non-tautological ethical rules—imperatives, principles of policy, aims, or however we may describe them—from statements of fact." '

But clearly 'ethical rules' are not synonymous with 'imperatives, principles of policy, etc.' 'Shut the door' is an imperative, but not an ethical rule. Perhaps most such imperatives that occur to one at first thought are, in some way, subordinate to ethical rules. But there is no logical contradiction in suggesting that there may be such imperatives or principles of policy which are of supra-ethical status. The biological imperative to eat comes nearly, but not quite, into this supra-ethical category. We can, with perfect logical consistency, conceive of an aim or principle of policy which, while not itself in its essence an ethical rule, would enable us to judge between different ethical rules. It is for such a principle that I am searching, and which I claim to be discoverable in the notion which I have referred to as 'biological wisdom'. Any such notion, once formulated, would of course almost certainly soon take on an ethical flavour, but this would be, as it were, acquired by infection from other ideas already existing within the mind of the person—an 'ethicizing being', let us remember—who entertained it. But in its essential logical nature, such a principle of policy would not be an ethical rule at all. It would be factual in derivation and non-ethical in character. The arguments of Hume and Moore against the derivation of ethical concepts from facts would not apply directly to it.

To a theory which attempted to discover a criterion for judging between ethical systems the refutation of the naturalistic fallacy would be largely beside the point. We should be denying Moore's[1] contention that 'the question, how "good" is to be defined, is the most fundamental question in all Ethics'. Instead

[1] *Principia Ethica*, p. 5.

our standpoint would be somewhat nearer to that ascribed to Kant by Broad,[1] when he wrote: 'Kant would say, I think, that it is no more the business of ethics to provide rules of conduct than is the business of logic to provide arguments. The business of ethics is to provide a test for rules of conduct, just as it is the business of logic to provide a test for argument.' But we should be carrying the argument one stage further. Where Kant was seeking to establish some particular ethical belief as a criterion by which to judge between alternative rules of conduct, we should be attempting to establish some general principle of wisdom as a criterion for judging between alternative ethical beliefs.

As a matter of fact, I am not certain whether I am prepared to accept the refutation of the naturalistic fallacy even in its application to the normal ethical concepts to which it is properly applicable. The validity of Hume's argument that one cannot logically proceed from an 'is' to an 'ought' depends entirely on what is the content of the notion conveyed by 'is'. If one conceives of existence as, to put it crudely, Newtonian space-time with some billiard balls flying round in it, then clearly neither 'ought' nor 'owes' nor many other concepts can be logically deduced. But if, to take another extreme, existence is considered as the manifestation of the nature of a beneficent Deity, quite other consequences would follow. In fact any invocation of 'is', other than as a logical copula, involves an epistemology, and it is impossible to reduce the relation of 'is' to 'ought' to a matter of pure logic. Again, Moore's argument that ethical concepts have a particular character which is non-natural and *sui generis* is based on an analysis by means of introspection of the language habits of adults. I question the adequacy of any analysis of such a restricted subject-matter. If we also take into consideration the formation of ethical notions in young children, we shall find, as I argued in 1941, that they arise from experiences of external phenomena, i.e. from something akin to facts—although such a complex interplay between intrinsic and extrinsic factors is involved that the concept of 'fact' is not very clear-cut in this connection.

[1] C. D. Broad, 1930, p. 123.

However, for my major purpose the validity or otherwise of the refutation of the naturalistic fallacy is irrelevant. I wish to maintain that it is possible to discuss, and perhaps to discover, a criterion which is not of an ethical nature, but is, if you wish, of a supra-ethical character; a criterion, that is to say, which would make it possible to decide whether a certain ethical system of values is in some definite and important sense preferable to another.

Now, it must be admitted that the relation between any supra-ethical criterion (let us call it 'wisdom') and ethical value is complex and not very easy to understand. Some might argue that ethical value is *ex officio* the overriding principle of policy, and can be judged only in terms of something else which has a still higher ethical value. 'What we cannot do,' says Nowell-Smith (p. 60), 'is to admit that our present moral code is in fact mistaken, for to admit this would be to abandon the moral view in question.' But to abandon the view would not necessarily be to deprive it of moral value. We can, I think, admit that the moral view which we have held up to date has turned out to be mistaken, and that we do not yet feel any positive ethical emotion towards the view which we are now persuaded is correct. Eventually we shall probably come to do so.

The ethical value which we shall attach to the new view of which we have been intellectually convinced may be at first only the kind of watered-down emotion which is all that the adult has freely at his disposal, and may fall far short of the powerful quasi-instinctive emotion which can be engendered so easily in early childhood. But the human psyche, even in adults, knows many peculiar processes. There are phenomena of conversion, in which extremely powerful emotions may become attached to notions which were previously regarded only coldly, or even rejected; or again ideas already charged with ethical feeling may become transformed, without losing their emotional importance, by the application of rational thought, which is after all not so impotent as a superficial acquaintance with modern psychology might suggest. We need not conclude that a supra-ethical criterion, even if non-ethical in its essential logical structure, must remain a pallid and insubstantial factor in our mental activities. Moore's question: 'Is wisdom (or whatever it may be) after all good?' would remain a real question (though one might query Moore's interpretation of 'good' as implying a character which is not only *sui generis* but also non-natural) but the question might at first be answered in the negative without markedly diminishing the importance of wisdom as a guide to action.

As an actual example of such a situation, consider the reaction of many people to the idea of the limitation of human fecundity. Many who have a feeling that it is ethically wrong to prevent births have also an intellectual, factually derived conviction that it is from some supra-ethical point of view desirable to do so; and they find themselves in process of transforming their ethical beliefs in this sense.

In my original essay of 1941 the fact that I was seeking an ethical criterion which would stand over and above the ethical beliefs of any single individual, and would enable one to judge between them, was not stated as clearly as it should have been. The criterion which we are here referring to as 'wisdom' was there included in the meanings of the ethical or the good, words which were used ambiguously, although they were usually qualified in some way when they were intended to be concerned with the general criterion rather than with individual ethical beliefs. For instance, towards the end of the original essay I wrote: 'We must accept the direction of evolution as good simply because it *is* good according to any realist definition of that concept.' Here the expression 'according to any realist definition of that concept'[1] was intended to show that the 'good' thus qualified referred not to the ideas considered good by any individual but to the general criterion by which ethical beliefs may be judged. Similarly, in the final summary I spoke of 'The ethical system which has a general validity for mankind as a whole'. This does not make it sufficiently clear that the criterion which I was seeking is not in its origin an ethical system of the same kind as are the ethical beliefs of particular men, but has

[1] This phrase is often omitted by critics who have referred to this sentence. Cf. Popper, *Poverty of Historicism*, p. 106, where misunderstanding is so complete that he regards the statement as merely the expression of an emotional attitude.

quite a different logical status, and is in fact an induction from the properties of individual ethical systems.

Owing to this unfortunate lack of clarity in exposition, and perhaps to the comparative novelty of the idea which was being put forward, the point has been misunderstood by almost everyone who has commented on the original thesis, both when they were friendly or when they were more severe critics. As an example of a hostile critic who has failed to appreciate the point I might refer to the most recent discussion of evolutionary ethics by Raphael. He quotes the beginning of the paragraph in which I make the remark given above, that the direction of evolution must be accepted as good simply because it is good according to any realist definition of that concept. In the rest of this paragraph I attempt to justify this statement by pointing out that in order to obtain a definition of the 'real good' (i.e. the criterion, 'wisdom') we have to look at the experience of the human world as a whole during its evolution rather than at any particular society. Raphael, however, quite failing to see that I am attempting to deduce a criterion which should transcend individual ethical beliefs, obviously does not see what the argument is that I am advancing. His quotation stops halfway through the train of thought. He proceeds to invent out of the blue the thesis that I am urging that 'people think good the way their society is going' and having erected this straw man he proceeds to demolish him.

Raphael's more fundamental criticism is expressed in the following paragraph, with which he brings to a conclusion his discussion of my views: 'Waddington thinks the answer to my question "What am I to do and for what reasons?" is the same as the answer to the question "What will I do and for what causes?" This is why he thinks that a causal account of how ethical judgments have come to be what they are can supply a criterion or rational ground for the ethical judgments we should make. But since the two questions and the kinds of answer they seek are of different logical types, Waddington's argument for using the direction of evolution as the direction for ethical judgments rests on a logical confusion.'

Here I take it that 'reasons' are verbal arguments deducible from some theory which accounts for certain phenomena in terms of the causal properties of the components of the system in which the phenomena occur. Any question about reasons has therefore a certain logical distinction from a question about causes, although once the latter question is answered, the reply to the former may be deducible from it. The more important point, however, is that Raphael phrases both questions with reference to an 'I', whereas my thesis would refer the second not to any particular individual but to some much larger entity, such as the human species, or even the living world as a whole. Raphael did not realize that I intended there to be a distinction between what I referred to as 'the ethical system of general validity' (which I am now referring to as wisdom) and the ethical beliefs of individual people. The difference between what he alleges I believe and what I was actually arguing may perhaps best be brought out if I rephrase his paragraph into a form in which I would accept it: 'Waddington thinks the answer to the question "What would it be wise for me to do and for what reasons?" can be deduced from the answer to the question: "What has the world at large been doing during its history and from what causes?" This is why he thinks that a causal account of how individual ethical judgments have come to be what they are can supply a criterion or rational ground for the judgment between different ethical beliefs which it is wise for us to make. These are two questions and the kinds of answer they seek are of different logical types. Waddington's argument for using the direction of evolution as the criterion for judgment between ethical beliefs rests on acceptance of this.'

Unfortunately, the point has also been missed by the most prominent supporter of the view that evolutionary progress has some bearing on ethical theory. Julian Huxley's well-known Romanes lecture, delivered in 1943, was published together with the lecture given by his grandfather fifty years earlier, with the title 'Evolution and Ethics'. Huxley, however, was not sufficiently careful to avoid a circular argument. He realized that we are seeking for a criterion to judge between ethical systems, but instead of finding this by some type of logical deduction not involving ethical valuation he suggested that we could use our existing ethical notions to recognize the criterion when it was

58

pointed out. He argues forcefully, and I think convincingly, for the fact that there is an overall direction recognizable in animal evolution, but he went on merely to *assert* that we can recognize this direction to be towards the good, and to urge that once we have made this recognition we can utilize our knowledge of the direction as a yardstick against which to measure any ethical valuation about which we may be in doubt. But this procedure is, as has been pointed out by his critics (e.g. Raphael), essentially circular. According to it, we would have to know what the criterion of ethical judgment should be before we could recognize it in the direction of evolution, and that direction would not then essentially transcend our individual ethical beliefs.

The manner in which I have suggested that one can establish a connection between the evolutionary process and ethical beliefs does not involve a circular argument of this kind. I argue that if we investigate by normal scientific methods the way in which the existence of ethical beliefs is involved in the causal nexus of the world's happenings, we shall be forced to conclude that the function of ethicizing is to mediate the progress of human evolution, a progress which now takes place mainly in the social and psychological sphere. We shall also find that this progress, in the world as a whole, exhibits a direction which is as well or ill defined as the concept of physiological health. Putting these two points together we can define a criterion which does not depend for its validity on any recognition by a pre-existing ethical belief.

We shall discuss in the following chapters the evidence for the two scientific hypotheses advanced—that the function of ethical beliefs is to mediate human evolution, and that evolution exhibits some recognizable direction of progress. The next philosophical topic which requires consideration is the concept of function.

CHAPTER 6

The Concept of Function

IN the discussion which followed the earlier presentation of this thesis, Broad[1] suggested that the notion of 'function' was the most critical point which required the attention of philosophers. His statement of the essential features of my argument was clear enough to be worth quoting in full. He wrote:

'I propose to state in my own way what it seemed to me that Dr Waddington really had in mind, as this gradually emerged in the course of the discussion. It is quite likely that I am to some extent misrepresenting him; but, if so, it is certainly not done with the intention of making an easy case against his views.

'(i) There is a certain group of interconnected emotions which may be called "ethical". Examples of these are moral approval and disapproval, feeling of guilt, feeling of obligation, and so on. An ethical belief is a belief which is toned with one or more of these emotions. Such emotions act as motives for or against doing actions towards which they are felt, and so we have specifically *moral* motivation.

'(ii) The study of young children shows that in the main ethical emotions become attached to actions which hinder or promote the adjustment of the child's social relations with his family in general and his parents in particular. He acquires a moral motive against doing the former and for doing the latter.

'(iii) A certain kind of ethical emotion becomes attached to a certain kind of action through the child doing such actions impulsively or instinctively and then finding that the reactions of his parents are satisfactory or unsatisfactory to him.

'(iv) From this we infer that the "function" of ethical emotions is to enable individuals to live in social relations with each

[1] 1943.

other; just as the "function" of the lungs is to aerate the blood, and that of the heart to distribute it throughout the body.

'(v) In particular cases a type of action which is detrimental to social harmony may have become associated with an approving ethical emotion, or one which would conduce to social harmony may have become associated with a disapproving ethical emotion. In such cases we say that ethical judgments about such actions are "false". This just *means* that these particular ethical judgments fail to perform that "function" which is characteristic of ethical judgments as a whole in human life. To call an ethical judgment "false" would be like calling a certain state or process in the heart or lungs "unhealthy" or "abnormal".

'(vi) A study of the genesis of ethical emotions and beliefs in the infant and of the part which they play in making family life possible *suggests* to us the function of such beliefs and emotions in the life of the race. But in order to determine the latter more precisely it is necessary to consider the main trend of change in social relations throughout human history. We then recognize that the "function" of ethical beliefs and emotions is to keep human social relations changing in this direction and to prevent them from deviating from it or reverting within it. To call a particular ethical belief "false", then, means that it fails to perform this, which is the characteristic function of ethical belief as such.

'I throw out this as a suggestion for critics of Dr Waddington to consider. I do not propose to criticize it myself here and now. But I would conclude by asking them to look with a very attentive eye at the notion of "function", which plays so large a part in my statement of the theory. I wonder whether this has not teleological and perhaps even ethical overtones which carry us beyond the methods and presuppositions of ordinary natural science.'

Now the first thing to note about the concept of function is this. The assertion that the function of A is the production of B does not imply that A always produces B. For instance, we may say that the function of the lungs is the oxygenation of the blood; but if the atmosphere happens to be nitrogen or some other gas, the blood will not be oxygenated but will be supplied with the gas that is present. Again, we say that the function of eating is to make possible normal growth and activity; but certain animals, at some time, may eat poison. Similarly, if we say that the function of the biological genetic system is to produce anagenetic evolutionary progress, and that of the human socio-genetic system is similar in connection with human evolution, this does not deny that both processes may also result in stasigenesis or evolutionary regression.[1]

When we assign a function to something, we in fact assert two propositions about it. Firstly, that it forms part of a causal network; and secondly, that the results of the causal network, when observed over the range in which they are expressed, exhibit some general property. Another way of expressing the latter point is to say that the causal network is organized. The concept of function is in fact very closely connected with that of organization, and can be regarded as a derivative of that more general notion. Is organization, then, an illegitimate concept? It probably is so in terms of a crudely mechanical materialist picture of the world, i.e. a picture in which we consider that all existing things can without loss be reduced to the movements and interactions of some ultimate constituent particles. But such a picture has never been more than a theoretical aspiration in biology, and is at present out of date even in the physical sciences. There are now, I think, few scientists who would consider it illegitimate to conclude that groups of elementary constituents may, by entering into close relationships with one another, build up complex entities which then enter into further causal interactions with one another *as units*. It is this fact, of the integration of groups of constituents into complexes, which in certain respects operate as units, which is spoken of as organization. In so far as it occurs, the concept of function is a legitimate one. If we have some complex entity A which acts as a unit, we can regard it as exhibiting organization of its constituent elements. Suppose that within A we can discern certain sub-units, P, Q, R, then the function of P within the organized system A is the contribution which P

---

[1] For a discussion of 'anagenesis', 'stasigenesis' and other technical terms concerned with evolutionary change, see Chapter 11.

makes towards those types of behaviour in which the unitary character of A is exhibited.

In discussing human ethical behaviour we are concerned with a realm in which the concept of organization would be in practice quite unavoidable at the present time, even by a mechanical materialist who was convinced that ultimately all phenomena should be completely reducible to the interplay of basic constituent elements. I do not wish at this time to go any further into this problem; any more than I intend to discuss at length the problem of free will. I will only point out, very briefly, that the latter problem seems usually to be discussed in terms which are not, in my opinion, the most relevant in connection with ethics. The question most commonly posed is, am I free to choose what I will do? For our ethical feelings a more crucial matter is the validity of our strivings. It would, surely, not be enough to be convinced that one is free to put out a hand and choose to pick up a pen rather than a pipe. It is when we have a strong sensation of making an effort of the will—when we are trying to screw out the last few foot-pounds at the end of a quarter-mile race, or to prevent ourselves giving utterance to that brilliant but nasty epigram we have just thought of about one of our colleagues—it is in circumstances of subjective effort that we are tempted to doubt the freedom of the will. It is the meaningfulness of this sense of effort that seems to be the essential problem. We have to see it, surely, as one end of a range which extends from quite unconscious activities, through conscious ones which involve only choices which involve no sense of dilemma, to matters which may pre-empt consciousness to the point of obsession.

As soon as one places the problem of free will in juxtaposition with that of consciousness, it becomes apparent that it cannot be solved either by any manipulation of our existing physico-chemical concepts, since these include no hint of self-awareness, or by any analysis of the language used in formulating the situation, since no linguistic analysis can annul our experience of self. We need ideas which depart more radically from those of the physical sciences; something perhaps akin to the thought of philosophers such as Spinoza and Whitehead, who have suggested that even non-living entities should not be denied qualities related to the self-awareness and will which we know, in. much more highly evolved forms, in ourselves. Some interesting speculations along these lines, from the special point of view of a biologist, have been published by Sinnott. I shall not, however, attempt any fuller discussion of them here. It seems to me that a readiness to discuss the problems of ethics implies an acceptance that some significance can be attached to the concepts of organization and of free will, and that anyone who wished to deny this should have closed this book after reading the title page.

CHAPTER 7

The Possibility of Evolutionary Theory

THE thesis I have proposed has involved the assumption that it is possible to discern in the results of evolution some general over-all direction of change which can truly be regarded as a special direction. The existence of such a direction has been asserted by many other authors, who have usually referred to it as the direction of evolutionary progress. This implies merely that a change in this direction has happened to occur, and that the direction is one which we are willing to recognize as progressive. I have, however, asserted, or at least implied, something rather more than this, namely that the direction is one which in some way arises as a result of the general structure of the universe; that is, it is not merely a direction in which progress happens to have occurred, but, in some of its aspects at least, it has the character of an inevitable consequence of the nature of the evolutionary process and the organisms involved in it. This assertion certainly requires discussion.

Evolution is a historical process. It affects every species of living being, and we are confronted on all sides with innumerable examples of the process in operation in particular organisms. Each of these instances is open to investigation, but there are two limitations on the kind of study which we can make of evolutionary processes.

In the first place, each individual instance of an evolutionary change is unique in that we cannot find another example of exactly the same change occurring for a second time. The developmental processes which occur in embryogenesis are in some ways comparable to the changes which happen during evolution, but we can easily find a batch of frogs' eggs each of which will develop in essentially the same way as all the rest, so that an experimental investigation can be repeated many times on similar material. This is impossible for evolutionary processes. The best we can hope for is to find a number of instances of rather similar evolutionary changes, which appear to share some feature in which we are particularly interested although differing in a considerable number of minor details.

Again, in the context of this book we are interested in the evolutionary process as a whole, and this is entirely unique in the sense that there is only one example of it, and we cannot find another which is even partially similar. These limitations are, of course, common to all historical study. They offer certain difficulties, but do not constitute an insuperable barrier to the causal understanding of evolutionary processes.

At least one authoritative philosophical writer, namely, Professor K. R. Popper, has, however, recently published a discussion which appears to deny the possibility of a rational understanding of historical changes in societies, and by extension of the changes in evolving animal populations. Popper emphasizes his own belief in the value of factual sociological investigations, but, in spite of this, in his discussion of other people's views he rarely deals with any single precise statement which they put forward, but tends to build up large all-embracing concepts which he regards as characterizing various schools of thought, which can then be categorized as a variety of 'isms'—historicism, naturalism and so on. He directs his attack primarily against the school which he names as 'holism'. All those who are particularly impressed by the organization of individual social or biological phenomena into organized groups are said to indulge in holistic thinking.

Popper states that they try to express their thought in terms of concepts such as 'society' or 'organism', which are supposed to embrace every conceivable aspect of the particular social population or living thing which is under investigation. This is perhaps a surprising claim. Perhaps the best known organismic or holistic thinker is A. N. Whitehead.[1] One of the central points of his thought was the distinction between events and objects. Events to Whitehead were entities of the kind that Popper seems

[1] I am thinking of the earlier works, such as *The Principles of Natural Knowledge* and *The Concept of Nature*.

to have in mind as typical of holistic thinking; but they were not concepts within the realm of thought, they were essentially existants. They could be considered as regions of external space-time; that is, something with which the human mind can grapple but which it can in principle not grasp in their entirety. The mistake of which Popper accuses the holists was in fact ruled out from the beginning. What the human intelligence does with a holistic event is to abstract from it certain particular aspects which can be conceptualized, and which are then known, in Whitehead's terminology, as objects. To mistake an object for an event is to commit what Whitehead called the 'fallacy of misplaced concreteness'.

Now it is, of course, very likely true that some writers about society have, to a greater or lesser extent, fallen into this trap. Without venturing myself to criticize authorities in a field in which I am an outsider, I can perhaps note that Hallowell[1] draws attention to Leslie White's 'culturology' as a 'logical extreme' of one type of thinking, for which 'culture becomes a continuum of extrasomatic elements. It moves in accordance with its own principles, its own laws; it is a thing *sui generis*. . . . Relative to the culture process the individual is neither creator nor determinant; he is merely a catalyst and a vehicle of expression'. But the fact that such notions are singled out for attention as extremes is sufficient indication that social scientists in general are well aware of the dangers of misplaced concreteness and cautious with regard to any views which might seem to approach them too nearly.

However, Popper accuses historians (and evolutionists) of trying to operate with concepts which would contain the whole essentially inexhaustible content of a holistic event, and thus of committing the fallacy which the most prominent 'historicist' particularly warned us against. He then advances the peculiar argument that, since one cannot attach any meaning to the notion of such an entity, therefore the whole idea of the direction of social or evolutionary change, or an understanding of the causes which bring it about, necessarily falls to the ground. His argument is stated as follows (p. 114):

[1] A. Irving Hallowell, note 22, quoting L. A. White, 1949 and 1950.

'Admittedly, any kind of change in a measurable social factor —for example, population growth—may be graphically represented as a track, just like the path of a moving body. But it is clear that such a diagram does not depict what people mean by the movement of society—considering that a stationary population may undergo a radical social upheaval. We may, of course, combine a number of such diagrams into one single multi-dimensional representation. But such a combined diagram cannot be said to represent the path of the movement of society; it does not tell us more than the single ones together; it does not represent any movement of "the whole society" but only changes of selected aspects. The idea that the movement of society itself —the idea that society, like a physical body, can move *as a whole* along a certain path and in a certain direction—is merely a holistic confusion.

'The hope, more especially, that we may some day find "the laws of motion of society", just as Newton found the laws of motion of physical bodies, is nothing but the result of these misunderstandings. Since there is no motion of society in any sense similar or analogous to the motion of physical bodies, there can be no such laws.'

Such persuasive force as this passage possesses depends upon three misunderstandings. The first is that referred to above; in point of fact very few authors, if any, are trying to conceptualize the event 'society'; nearly all writers are concerned only with an object 'society', that is to say, with certain abstracted aspects of the fully concrete existant which occurs externally to the observer. The second misunderstanding arises—or at least can easily arise—from the attempt to make an analogy with the motion of a physical body. This tends to produce a mental picture of something like a billiard ball moving over an area. But this is not by any means the only sort of phenomenon which goes on in the inanimate world. We can very easily find physical happenings which present a much closer analogy to what is meant by the direction of social or evolutionary change. Suppose we mix two substrate molecules ab and cd with two enzymes P and Q, which respectively split the substrates into a and b, and c and d; and suppose that c acts as inhibitor of the enzyme P; then the chemical constitution of the mixture will gradually change in a defined way which can be worked out mathematically. This set of changes could be expressed as the movement of a point in a multidimensional phase-space. I do not see that even the strictest adherent to the purity of the English language could object to the use of the word 'motion' in this connection, or to our speaking of the existence of a path along which the movement of the system proceeds. It is in a sense analogous to this that one speaks of an evolutionary path or a direction of evolutionary (or developmental) change; and it is clear, to return to the former point, that such a manner of speaking does not in any way involve an attempt to conceptualize the existant system as a whole. For instance, we can speak of the path along which the enzyme-substrate system changes without paying any attention whatever to any alterations in the colour of the solution which may be occurring at the same time.

Finally, it is a mistake to suppose that Newton's laws apply to physical bodies, in the sense of the actual material things which we encounter in everyday experience. The laws of physics apply to entities which have been given precise definitions which, in the case of conventional Newtonian dynamics, involve such notions as infinite hardness and location of mass at a point. These entities are never existents in the same sense as actual billiard balls or inclined planes are. They are, in Whitehead's terminology, 'scientific objects', and no less so than the scientific object 'a given society' which may be studied by a sociologist or 'a given evolutionary sequence' which may be investigated by a biologist.

Popper's book is dedicated to 'the countless men and women . . . who fell victims to the fascist and communist belief in Inexorable Laws of Historical Destiny'. This bespeaks wholly admirable sentiments, but one can hardly agree that in order to controvert certain false political arguments it is necessary to reject, as Popper wishes to, all possibility of understanding historical or evolutionary processes. Major philosophical generalizations are blunderbuss weapons, too undiscriminating to be properly employed in such a context.

We may conclude, I think, that the concept of a direction of evolutionary change is a legitimate one. It does not, of course, follow that we can necessarily in practice discern such a direction.

But before discussing this, which we shall do in Chapter 11, there is another argument of Popper's which requires notice.

Popper points out that any alleged understanding of a historical process such as evolution, if it is to be more than the discernment of a mere contingent trend that might be reversed at any time, would make it possible to predict, in some degree at least, the course of future events. Now he claims to have shown by rigid logical argument that any such prediction is inherently impossible. In its most general form his argument is to the effect that 'no scientific predictor can possibly predict by scientific methods its own future results'. In a more specific form the gist of the argument is contained in the three propositions: '(1) The course of human history is strongly influenced by the growth of human knowledge. (2) We cannot predict by rational or scientific methods the future growth of our scientific knowledge. (3) We cannot therefore predict the future course of human history.'

These arguments are exceedingly abstract, and their cogency depends entirely on what is meant by a predictor, or what degree of precision we feel must be involved before a statement about the future can qualify as a prediction. Professor Popper, I think, envisages the predictor as an apparatus which is set up once for all and remains thereafter unchanged. We might, however, consider the predictor capable of learning, that is to say, of improvement as time goes on. Indeed, if arguments about a predictor are to be used to justify statements about human understanding of history, or about the evolutionary system, we certainly must allow for the possibility of the predictor learning, since as we shall see, both the genetic system and the evolutionary system are subject to selective pressures which result in their improvement. Now, if a predictor learns, it may still remain unable to predict what its future predictions will be in detail, but it can certainly predict that they will be more reliable than its present predictions. This provides a satisfactory analogy for the type of conclusion about the course of evolution which I shall advance below, namely, that there is an inherent tendency for the efficiency of the evolutionary system to be improved. Popper's argument therefore does not make it illegitimate to discuss evolution in the terms which I shall be using later.

CHAPTER 8

The Shape of Biological Thought; or the
Virtues of Vicious Circles

THE disagreement or even distaste and scorn which many modern philosophers evince towards theories such as I am putting forward here probably have their origin in rather deep-lying disagreements about what constitutes a convincing argument. Philosophical thinkers have, in the last few decades, been profoundly influenced by many advances in modern science. The advances which have made most impression on them have been those in the physical sciences. Open any book of the present day dealing with epistemology or the general problems of philosophy, and you will find a discussion of pointer readings, the theory of relativity, the quantum theory, the indeterminacy principle, and so on. These are undoubtedly exceedingly important matters, but one would have thought them somewhat remote from the general activities of human beings, except in the very special field of the quantitative analysis of the behaviour of material bodies. Man is, after all, a biological entity. It is only in his most generalized characteristics, which he shares with sticks and stones, that he is a part of the subject matter of physics or chemistry. In his full being—or at least if we do not wish to beg the question, over a much wider range of his being—he falls within the province of biology. There are three currents of thought arising within biology which seem to me much more relevant to epistemology and general philosophy than anything that physics has or could discover about the behaviour of the ultimate units into which matter can be analysed. Two of these points relate to the subject matter of thought; the third to its logical structure.

The first unavoidable biological fact is that of evolution. For at least the last hundred years, since Darwin wrote, biologists have had to consider all living things, including man, as being produced by a process of evolution which operates in such a way as to bring its results into adjustment to the circumstances surrounding it. It is by now absolutely conventional and a matter of first principles to consider the whole physiological and sensory apparatus of any living thing as the result of a process which tailors it into conformity with the situations with which the organism will have to deal. The same principle undoubtedly applies to behavioural characteristics, and there is no obvious reason to deny it out of hand in relation to intellectual and even moral characteristics in those organisms which exhibit them. Within the professional field of biology there is a very general recognition of the occurrence of evolution of types of thinking, and of behaviour patterns, including behaviour to which we attribute a moral value. For instance, Roe and Simpson have recently edited a large symposium on *Evolution and Behaviour*; and we find such eminent biologists as J. B. S. Haldane and H. J. Muller discussing the technical genetical problems involved in the evolution of moral quantities.

The second major contribution of modern biology to the way in which we envisage living things derives from its emphasis on the importance of individual development. A few decades ago the growing point of biological thought was the analysis of the operatons of the living machine. The most advanced biology dealt with problems of metabolism, of the intake of oxygen, foodstuffs, etc., the changes they undergo in the body, and their final excretion, together with problems of co-ordination between activities going on in different regions of the body. The fundamental problem of biology was seen as the understanding of the nature of enzyme action. More recently we have seen an increasing importance attached to questions concerning the mechanisms by which the functioning apparatus becomes gradually transformed as the individual develops from the fertilized egg onwards. This movement of thought, which had its origins in the work of such men as His, Roux, Driesch and Spemann, eventually and inevitably became linked with concepts derived from genetics. Its full depth and profundity then became apparent.

The dominant position it now holds within the technical field of biology may be recognized in the fact that almost any biologist nowadays would admit that the crucial problem for theoretical biology is an understanding of the way in which genes control the characters of the organisms which develop from newly fertilized zygotes. The biology of metabolic systems can in some ways be compared to physics and chemistry in the days of the Daltonian irreducible atoms. The serious introduction of developmental thought introduces a new dimension, in much the same way as the Bohr-Rutherford atomic model opened new vistas for the physical sciences.

Both these new types of biological subject matter—the evolutionary and the developmental—have called for a new type of thinking, a type for which the most convincing causal structure is a circular one, in which A influences B and B again influences A.

I will return to the point of logical structure later, but, prior to and independent of any conclusions we may reach about it, I should like to emphasize that, however they may be thought about, the facts of evolution and development simply cannot be omitted from any discussion of the human condition which hopes to carry conviction at the present time; and yet, in spite of the publicity which is given to Darwin, they are very generally neglected by thinkers who are not professional biologists. H. J. Muller has recently published a paper with a somewhat angry title 'A Hundred Years Without Darwin Are Enough'. He was not thinking of epistemologists and philosophers, but he well might have been. Remarkably few professional philosophers of the present day so much as mention the fact that the human sensory and intellectual apparatus has been brought into being by an evolutionary process whose observed effects in all other instances are to produce operative systems conformable to the situations with which they will have to deal. Take two examples more or less at random: the word evolution does not occur in the index of either Gilbert Ryle's *The Concept of Mind* or A. J. Ayer's *The Problem of Knowledge*. To the biologist, I think it is bound to remain almost inconceivable that one can talk much sense about the relation between man and the external world if one leaves out of account the fact that man has been brought into being by evolution in relation to the external world. This is not to deny, of course, that many different interpretations of the situation might be possible in place of the particular interpretation that I am offering here. But even if one were to finish up by concluding, for instance, that evolution had not occurred in the human epistemological apparatus—even if one were to retreat to the pre-scientific concept of man as a special creation, springing fully-armed from the head of his creator—the presupposition that evolution has affected him is so strong that it needs special arguments and not mere silence for its rejection.

This does not imply, of course, that evolutionary processes have already supplied mankind with an intellectual apparatus which is perfectly efficient in dealing with the external world. As we shall see later (Chapter 13), our stock has evolved a socio-genetic mechanism for transmitting information down the generations which, although much more effective than anything which preceded it, exhibits many obvious defects. It is clear also that our sensory apparatus also offers many opportunities for improvement, for instance, in discriminating scents, in visual accuity at small dimensions, or in responding to a broader spectrum of electro-magnetic vibrations. There can be no reason to doubt that our conceptualizing and logical faculties might also be susceptible of betterment. Indeed it seems probable that the progress of experimental physics has brought us in contact with phenomena to which our mental apparatus is not at all well suited, so that we find it exceedingly difficult to formulate a structure of concepts which corresponds to the facts. The point is, however, not that evolution produces perfect instruments for coping with all conceivable aspects of the world, but that the active systems it brings into being must have at least sufficient effectiveness to 'get by' in the circumstances of life in which they are used. There must be some correspondence, of a degree which requires notice and not neglect, between the structure of our mental activities and the structure of our environment.

Here is one example typical of many in modern philosophical works in which a train of thought seems to call out for the invocation of evolutionary ideas but in which they fail to appear. Consider the following lines from Hannah Arendt's recent, most stimulating and in many ways profound book *The Human Con-dition* (p. 288): 'In other words, the world of the experiment seems always capable of becoming a man-made reality, and this, while it may increase man's power of making and acting, even of creating a world, far beyond what any previous age dared to imagine in dream and fantasy, unfortunately puts man back once more—and now even more forcefully—into the prison of his own mind, into the limitations of patterns he himself created. The moment he wants what all ages before him were capable of achieving, that is, to experience the reality of what he himself is not, he will find that nature and the universe "escape him" and that a universe construed according to the behaviour of nature in the experiment and in accordance with the very principles which man can translate technically into a working reality lacks all possible representation. . . . It is therefore not surprising that the universe is not only "practically inaccessible but not even thinkable", for "however we think it", it is wrong; not perhaps quite as meaningless as "triangular circle" but much more so than a "winged lion".' Here the phrases such as 'the prison of his own mind', 'the limitations of patterns he himself created', 'to experience the reality of what he himself is not', all imply that one can conceive of a radical distinction between man and the rest of nature. They presuppose the possibility of considering man as a being created independently of the rest of the world, which he observes and acts on as something essentially foreign to himself. They leave out of account altogether the fact of evolution, the fact that the faculty by which man creates patterns to fit the natural world has itself been brought into being by a process which has moulded that faculty in such a way that it has the ability to form patterns which are in some way appropriate to what it has to deal with.

In the last sentence quoted from Miss Arendt above, she is herself quoting from the eminent physicist Erwin Schroedinger (1952). It is true indeed that eminent physicists have proved no less unaware of the consequences of accepting an evolutionary origin for man than have the philosophers. Schroedinger closes another book of his (1954) with the words 'For the purpose of constructing the picture of the external world, we have used the greatly simplifying device of cutting our own personality out, removing it. . . . This is the reason why the scientific world view contains of itself no ethical values, no aesthetic values, not a word about our own ultimate scope or destination, and no God, if you please'. This puts very succinctly one side of the paradox into which non-evolutionary thinking has fallen. The other side is equally clearly stated by another eminent theoretical physicist, also quoted by Hannah Arendt, namely, Walter Heisenberg (pp. 22-3. Arendt quotes the same passage on her p. 261). Heisenberg writes: 'If, starting from the conditions of modern science, we try to find out where the bases have started to shift we get the impression that it would not be too crude an over-simplification to say that *for the first time in the course of history, modern man on this earth now confronts himself alone, and that he no longer has partners or opponents.* . . . Thus even in science, the object of research is no longer nature itself, but man's investigation of nature. Here, again, man confronts himself alone.'

Thus, while Schroedinger suggests that we have left man wholly out of our picture of nature, Heisenberg argues that we have nothing but man included in it. Surely it is clear that the paradox arises as a consequence of the attempt to draw a distinction between man and nature of a more ultimate kind than the facts warrant. Man is a part of nature, he forms a certain picture of what we may crudely call the external world, not as an outside observer of it but just because the forces of the external world have moulded his evolution into a being capable of reflecting it in a way adequate for carrying on the activities of life. We can, I think, be quite confident of this statement in relation to the physiological, sensory and intellectual capacities of man for handling his environment. Theologians might wish to reserve a small but crucial element in the human constitution outside the sphere of relevance of evolution. Such a thesis cannot be rejected out of hand, but it requires special arguments to support it. The great bulk of human nature, and the part that is most easy to observe, has undoubtedly been produced by evolution, and has been moulded by the necessity to interact reasonably successfully with the non-human components of the universe.

Such a point of view has of course many implications for questions of general epistemology. It implies, for instance, that we have a mind capable of grasping logical structures because the universe exhibits regularities which make logical thinking a useful activity. It has implications also for the theory of perception. It argues that we experience tables and chairs, and not only (if at all) mere sense data, because it is evolutionarily useful to perceive, as Whitehead put it (1928), in the mode of causal efficacy as well as in that of presentational immediacy. Dewey, of course, explored some of these ideas, not always very convincingly. But I do not wish, even if I were capable of doing so, to pursue here the complex ramifications of this line of thought into these fields.

The point I wish to make is that also in the context of the evaluation of ethical systems it is inadmissible to try to erect a firm dualism between man and nature. When, for instance, Ewing writes (p. 74): 'There is nothing logically absurd about the supposition that the whole evolutionary process was harmful, and that it would have been better if life had never develeopd beyond its first stage or any intermediate stage we might happen to fancy', his contention cannot in my opinion be accepted. One is bound to ask 'harmful to whom?' If we could conceive of man outside the evolutionary process, and in possession of a logic unrelated to the rest of the universe, Ewing's conclusion might follow; but if harmfulness is to be assessed entirely from the point of view of the products of evolution, and without bringing in any exterior, non-evolutionary point of reference, it is I think illogical (in the sense of being a contradiction in terms) to suppose that the whole evolutionary process is harmful.

Again, when Emmet writes: 'It will not do to call a world outlook "scientific" because it can bring natural and ethical phenomena under the same concepts, if those concepts were in fact derived from analogies with human actions and purposes in the first place and read back into the natural world. The concept of "evolutionary progress" may be a case in point'; she is once again basing her thought on the implicit assumption that human actions and purposes could be something completely external to, and independent of, the natural world. The same assumption again underlies this quotation from Arendt (p. 293): 'The conviction that objective truth is not given to man but that he can know only what he makes himself is not the result of scepticism but of a demonstrable discovery,[1] and therefore does not lead to resignation but either to redoubled activity or to despair. The world loss of modern philosophy, whose introspection discovered consciousness as the inner sense with which one senses his senses and found it to be the only guarantee of reality, is different not only in degree from the age-old suspicion of the philosophers towards the world and towards the others with whom they shared the world; the philosopher no longer turns from the world of deceptive perishability to another world of eternal truth, but turns away from both and withdraws into himself.' Again, what the biologist notices is that the philosopher is not supposed to turn to himself as one constituent of the world, someone who not only makes it himself but is himself made by it. Arendt, who has just been discussing Cartesian doubt, is still caught by what Whitehead called the Cartesian dualism. Her philosopher is a would-be quite independent observer set over against the world. To any evolutionist he must appear as merely one part of it.

An outlook which sees the human observer as something quite separate and distinct from the external world which he perceives finds a sympathetic logical form in relations between two clearly separable terms, and a congruous type of causal analysis in statements such as that A causes B. For a more biological outlook, which sees man as simultaneously an observer, and a product, of the remainder of the world, such simple logical and causal structures are not adequate. For those who feel at home in the climate of present-day biology, a statement such as that A causes B inevitably has an air of incompleteness. What causes A, and what effects does B have? The system is not complete but leaves loose ends, which can only be tidied away by inventing something outside the system.

We feel more confident in an analysis which arrives at a conclusion of the form that A has a causal influence on B and B has a causal influence on A. In recent years, such circular causal systems have been referred to by the fashionable term 'feedback', borrowed from engineering, and the word cybernetics has been

[1] She was referring to Galileo's telescope.

introduced as a general term to cover the study of properties of systems organized in this manner; but this type of thinking has a much longer history in biology than this special terminology, and a much wider reference than the quantitative analysis of the operation of various material systems to which cybernetic ideas are usually applied. The general point is the replacement of sequences of simple causal or logical relations by organized causal or logical networks, which ideally and when complete should be self-contained, in the sense that they necessitate no reference to anything outside the system.

Theories which involve such self-contained and organized causal networks may easily be taken to be no more than vicious circles. For instance, Arendt writes[1] that it seems that science 'has fallen into a vicious circle, which can be formulated as follows: scientists formulate their hypotheses to arrange their experiments and then use these experiments to verify their hypotheses; during this whole enterprise, they obviously deal with a hypothetical nature'. But, one asks, if the experiments *do* verify the hypotheses, what more could one want? To call the nature with which the scientists deal 'hypothetical'—is this any more than to make a depreciatory emotional noise about it? If science can produce—and this is its aim, never of course finally to be attained—a closed but consistent causal network in which the scientist himself is included, can any meaning be attached to a demand for something more?

Although some types of circularity in causal organization appear more convincing than mere open-ended causal sequences, it cannot of course be denied that certain other types of circular argument merit being dismissed as vicious circles. If, for instance, one says, as Herbert Spencer did and probably Julian Huxley also, that evolutionary progress is good and therefore the good can be defined by means of evolutionary progress, the argument does not escape from the imputation of being a mere vicious circle. The second clause, that good can be defined from evolutionary progress, adds nothing whatever to the first, which states that evolutionary progress is good.

It is very necessary to distinguish a circular argument which

[1] H. Arendt, *loc. cit.*, p. 287.

is 'vicious' in the usual sense from one which validly expresses the structure of a causally organized system. The basic distinction can perhaps be expressed as follows. Consider two terms A and B. A vicious circle arises if we attribute some property to A, or claim that some sub-systems within A produce an attribute which belongs to A as a whole, and from these premises attempt to deduce some character of B. The viciousness arises from the fact that B has not been essentially referred to in the premises. For instance, if we say that goodness is an attribute of evolutionary progress (which would correspond to A), we cannot use this to make deductions about anything other than evolutionary progress, for instance, about human life (which would correspond to B). On the other hand, a valid circular statement of causal organization is of the form that A conditions the appearance of an attribute of B, and that B produces an attribute of A. Thus one does not commit any logical fallacy, but instead exhibits the real structure of the situation, if one says that nature through the processes of evolution has produced in the human race a certain perceptive-intellectual apparatus (influence of A on B), that this apparatus sees nature in a particular way (influence of B on A). Moreover, such an organized causal system is not necessarily, or even usually, stable in time. If at any moment A influences B, that is quite likely to change the manner in which B is acting on A, so that the system as a whole will become modified as time passes. The scientist, for instance, on the basis of the way in which he now sees nature will formulate hypotheses as to how he might see it more fully; and when he carries out experiments he offers nature the opportunity to influence him and his world view. It is this type of argument which has here been applied to ethics. The processes of evolution have produced the phenomenon that the human race entertains ethical beliefs. Man can then, not so much through experiment but rather by taking account of its results, use evolution to guide the way in which those beliefs will develop in the future.

The temporal instability of organized causal systems is one of their most important properties and it will be advisable to discuss it somewhat further. Much of the thought devoted to cybernetics has been in the context of various mechanical devices designed by man. In these, circular causal systems (systems involving feedback) have been designed for the specific purpose of changing in time in such a way as to attain some pre-set goal. The theory of their operation usually involves the concept of 'negative feedback'; that is to say, the input into some part of the machine of an influence (for instance, an electric or mechanical force) whose value is a function of the difference between the present state of the machine and its pre-designed end. The invocation of a pre-designed end-point is, however, not at all a necessary part of an analysis into a closed causal organization. For instance, if we mix together definite quantities of a certain number of chemical substances, all of which are capable of interacting with one another, the mixture as a whole will form a causal system which will change in time until it reaches a certain equilibrium constitution. In the biological field, progressive changes of this kind form the major subject matter of the study of embryonic development.

A fertilized egg is provided with a certain number of genes in its nucleus and an organized structure of different regions of cytoplasm. The genes influence the cytoplasm by controlling the specificity of the substances which are synthesized within it; and the different regions of cytoplasm affect these gene-directed processes by controlling the relative rates at which they proceed. The system as a whole changes along a defined and recognizable course as time passes. Such a time-trajectory of developmental change arises from the characteristics of the closed circular causal organization of the system of genes and cytoplasm, but its mechanism does not involve anything strictly comparable to a 'negative feedback', dependent on a predetermined end-point—a concept which biologists would consider teleological and therefore inadmissible. I have proposed (1952) the word 'creode', derived from the Greek words χρη 'necessity' and ὸδοσ 'a path' as a name for such time-trajectories of progressive developmental change, which arise from the nature of the causal organization of their starting-point.

Although the concept was first derived in an embryological context, creodes are a type of phenomena which occur in many other fields also. For instance, although the course of any particular evolutionary lineage cannot usually be considered a creode, since it is dependent perhaps on chance and on external environmental circumstances which may not be fully determined at the beginning of the evolutionary process, yet certain aspects of evolution as a whole do probably show the essential features of creodes. They are found, for instance, in the evolution of genetic systems as proposed by Darlington and discussed more fully on p. 101. If there is as I suggest on p. 102 an evolution of evolutionary systems, this also would be a creodic phenomenon.

The importance of developmental considerations was the third of the biological currents of thought to which attention was drawn at the beginning of this chapter. Any characteristic of a living organism must be thought of not only as something which has a functional role in the life of the organism, and not only as something which has been evolved through a considerable course of history, but also as something which undergoes a process of development during the individual lifetime of the organism. The concepts which have been derived from the scientific study of development are no less relevant to philosophical thought than those of evolutionary theory; and no consideration of the attributes or faculties of mankind can be accepted as satisfactory which neglects these two routes by which biology approaches the problems presented by living things. The inadequacy of the fashionable method of linguistic analysis in this respect has already been pointed out in Chapter 4.

CHAPTER 9

The Biological Evolutionary System

THE world of living things, in which evolution has occurred, is
enormously complex. It contains at the present day representatives of very ancient and simple types of organism, which have
persisted almost unchanged from the earliest times of which we
have knowledge, and it contains others whose evolutionary history has involved very considerable changes in the quite recent
past. When we study such records as we have of the paths along
which evolutionary changes have proceeded, we find what at
first looks like an almost inextricable jumble of different types of
events. Some lines of change have led to increases in complexity,
others to simplifications. Sequences of changes which at first
seem to fall into a single series along one well-defined line
become resolved with further knowledge into a group of inter-
lacing paths rather than a single one. Some paths persist only a
short time and then come to a stop with the extinction of the
species in question. Others continue for some period towards,
for instance, a greater complexity of structure, only later to have
their direction reversed, and then lead to a greater simplification.
Yet, in spite of this complexity of detail, almost all biologists
who have professionally studied the subject come to the conclusion that it is possible to discover a pattern in evolution as a
whole—a general direction in which the process has, on the
whole, proceeded—so that it is not meaningless to speak of
certain organisms as being more highly evolved than others.
This conclusion in fact antedates even the theory of evolution
itself. It was enshrined in the late mediaeval concept of the
Great Ladder of Being, which was considered to be a static
orderly arrangement of unchanging types of living things into
a natural hierarchy which led from the simplest up to the highest,

84

and eventually through man further still into the realm of the angels.[1]

Many recent biologists have described the nature of this main trend which defines the direction of evolutionary progress. It is, in the first place, a phenomenon which can be exhibited; it can be defined ostensively, by taking someone to a museum or opening a good text-book of comparative anatomy and pointing to the examples of the animals required to illustrate the point. If this were all one could say about it the course of evolution would remain a mere contingent happening. It would just be the case that the main path of evolution happened to be in this direction, although it might equally have been in some other. Even if that were all, the direction which it had proceeded would obviously be a fact of enormous importance about the world.

However, that is certainly not all that can be said about the situation; although as one tries to proceed further, to formulate in general terms the character of evolutionary progress and to relate it to the nature of the evolutionary forces, one enters into more difficult and debatable ground. One point on which there seems general agreement is that the evolutionary step by which man has become differentiated from his precursors involves something more than a mere contingent set of happenings which might equally well have taken a different form. On the contrary, as Huxley,[2] for instance, has argued in detail, man has a series of characteristics which would seem to be inescapably demanded by any being capable of transcending, as he has done, the animal mechanism of evolutionary advance. Although Huxley enumerated a number of these characteristics, such as adequate size, a long period of growth, a homeostatic internal environment and so on, he did not very convincingly succeed in defining the general characteristics of evolutionary progress in a form which would apply both to the sub-human and to the human world. We can now, I think, make somewhat more progress in doing so, and can at least tentatively point to those aspects of the evolutionary processes which have rendered it inevitable that evolu-

[1] See Lovejoy, Tillyard.
[2] 1941.

tionary changes of the general kind that we recognize as progressive must occur.

The major advance in the theory of biological evolution since Darwin's day has been the rise of Mendelian genetics. It is hardly an exaggeration to say that when Darwin wrote biology possessed no theory of inheritance. Since then, the existence of more or less discrete hereditary factors has been discovered, their position in the cell ascertained to be on the chromosomes in the nucleus, and, the behaviour of these chromosomes analysed in great detail both in normal and in various more or less unusual conditions. In fact the phenomena of heredity have been investigated in such minute detail that we are now passing out of the, as it were, 'Dalton' phase, in which the genes appeared to be completely separate and discrete, into a 'Rutherford' phase in which we can profitably discuss sub-genic structure.

The whole of this complex of phenomena which are concerned with the manner in which hereditary determinants are passed on from one generation to the next may be referred to as the 'genetic system'. From the point of view of evolutionary theory three main points have emerged concerning it. The first is that the existence of discrete hereditary determinants safeguards variation against being lost if dissimilar animals cross breed as Darwin feared it might. Indeed the fact that during the greater part of the life cycle of most animals and plants the hereditary factors are present in the diploid condition implies that most organisms carry within them much greater potentialities for variation in their offspring than would appear at first sight. The second point, which is one that we owe primarily to the insight of Darlington, is that the genetic system itself can be regarded not only as an agent but also as a subject of evolutionary change, which is to say that the genetic system itself evolves. This I shall return to later.

The third point concerns the origin of new variation. It is essential to any theory of evolution that there must be some mechanism by which new variation is brought into being. Darwin was driven to speculate as to what this mechanism might be. In the absence of any understanding of how hereditary qualities are transmitted, he made no pretence that he had found a solution

86

fully satisfactory to himself, although he was somewhat tempted by the theory, usually associated with the name of Lamarck, that characters acquired by organisms in the course of their lifetime might be transmitted to their offspring. Later experimental investigations have shown that in general this is not so. In quite recent years, a few special cases have been discovered, for instance, in the transformation of bacteria and the induction of specific enzyme synthesis in relation to corresponding substrates, which could, with some stretching of the terminology, be interpreted as cases of the inheritance of acquired characters. But these not only require very specialized and particular conditions to bring them about, but even when variability can be induced in such ways, there are several reasons why the processes involved do not seem able to fill the role in evolutionary theory for which the doctrine of the inheritance of acquired characters was originally designed.

We are still confronted with an enormous range of phenomena which look as though they would be much more easily explained in terms of the inheritance of acquired characters than in any other way, but the overwhelming concensus of opinion in the biological world is that the facts preclude us from adopting this simple mode of explanation. Our knowledge of the genetic system, which is very extensive and detailed, forces us to the conclusion that the origin of new hereditary variation is to be found only in alterations and rearrangements of the atomic groupings out of which the hereditary factors of the chromosomes are composed. These alterations take place either spontaneously or under the influence of disturbing ionizations or chemical reactions, and in doing so follow rules of stability which are still entirely unknown to us, but which must be properties of the heredity molecules themselves and have little or no relation to the precipitating events by which the alterations were stimulated. For all such alterations and rearrangements of the hereditary substance, the general name 'mutation' is used, and one of the most firmly based doctrines of modern genetics is that mutation is a random process. I do not wish to challenge this, but I shall suggest later that some care is necessary in interpreting the word random.

In the present day biology evolution is envisaged as resulting from the interaction between, on the one hand, the genetic system characterized by random mutation, and on the other, natural selection. The concept of natural selection was for some time obscured by some of the phrases, such as 'survival of the fittest', invented by Darwin's contemporaries in the course of polemics against those who wished to reject the evolutionary hypothesis. More dispassionate analysis has led to the general realization that the crucial matter is not survival but hereditary transmission, and that those individuals that are successful in transmitting hereditary qualities to offspring are not necessarily 'fitter' than their competitors in any other respect than just in success in doing so. Natural selection is in fact a truism, but one which had to be pointed out before it was recognized.

Most biologists at the present day, in expounding evolutionary theory, seem to be content to leave it that the mechanism by which evolution has been brought about is composed of these two major factors: the genetic system with random mutation on the one hand and natural selection on the other. The evolutionary pressures exerted by these two factors are exhibited as being quite external to the nature of the organisms involved. The essential evolutionary pressure exerted by the genetic system is that of mutation, and mutation, it is explained, is a random process. Any explanation which might be offered for the nature of the mutational changes would have to be found, it is asserted, in the chemical composition of the genes and not in the nature of the complete biological organism in which these genes are carried. Mutation thus appears as essentially an external force to which the organism passively submits. Again, natural selective pressures are usually thought of as arising simply from the external environment. When the climate changes, a new predator appears, or industrial fumes blacken the tree trunk on which the animal lives, the populations of organisms concerned cannot, it is usually implied, do anything but submit to these pressures and wait until the equally uncontrollable process of mutation throws up a new hereditary variant which enables them to meet the environment's challenge more successfully.

It is as though in one part of a quarry mutation led to the

mixing together of stones of many different sizes, while in another part the mixture was thrown on to a series of sorting sieves which finally let through only those within a certain range.

Now, with such a mechanism—random mutation in selective but unresponsive environments—it would appear difficult to find any principle which would produce any specific direction of evolutionary change. All evolution would appear to be purely a contingent phenomenon, which just happened to go in the way that it did, but for no ascertainable reason. One could admit, of course, that the mechanism of natural selection is one which will, as has been frequently pointed out, produce states of extreme improbability by preserving just those particular chance variations which happen to fit in with the environment and rejecting all others, but there seems at first sight to be nothing which could decide as to which state of improbability will be favoured in this way out of all those which might conceivably be possible.

In my opinion, biology has already made all the discoveries of matters of principle which can be reached by this way of formulating the situation. The time seems to have come when we need to take into account two further aspects of the evolutionary mechanism.[1] In the first place, natural selective pressures impinge not on the hereditary factors themselves, but on the organisms as they develop from fertilized eggs to reproductive adults. It is only by a piece of shorthand, convenient for mathematical treatments, that indices of selective value are commonly attached to individual genes. In reality we need to bring into the picture not only the genetic system by which hereditary information is passed on from one generation to the next, but the 'epigenetic system' by which the information contained in the fertilized egg is translated into the functioning structure of the reproducing individual. As soon as one begins to think about the development of the individuals in an evolving population, one realizes that each organism during its lifetime will respond in some manner to the environmental stresses to which it is submitted, and in a population there is almost certain to be some genetic variation in the intensity and character of these responses.

[1] Cf. Waddington, 1957.

Natural selection will favour those individuals in which the responses are of most adaptive value.

Two consequences can be expected to follow, and have in fact been demonstrated experimentally. In the first place natural selection will build up genotypes which set going developmental mechanisms which easily respond to environmental stresses by the production of a well-organized modification which is of adaptive value. It will, as it were, build into the genotype a gun which is not only set on a hair trigger but which is aimed to hit the target when it goes off. In so far as such a developmental response becomes precisely delimited and easily initiated, it becomes the more likely to be produced by unspecified changes in the chemical nature of the hereditary substance. Mutations, which we can think of as random when we are considering nucleoproteins in the chromosomes, will have effects on the phenotype of the organisms which are not necessarily random, but which will be modified by the types of instability which have been built into their epigenetic mechanisms by selection for response to environmental stresses.

Since this is an unfamiliar point of view it may be as well to illustrate it by actual example. If eggs of the fruitfly Drosophila are submitted to ether vapour shortly after laying, a proportion of them tend to have their development modified so that they produce a very peculiar phenotype, known as bithorax, in which the third segment of the thorax of the animal is transformed from its normal small and obscure structure into a duplicate of the large second thoracic segment. This modification is, of course, of no adaptive value, and the environmental stress is not one which Drosophila are likely to meet in the normal circumstances of evolution. However, for the purposes of an experiment designed to illustrate general principles, we can treat the response as though it were favoured by selection, and in each generation breed from those individuals in the population which respond to the stress in this way. When this was done with a population taken from a normal wild type stock, it became apparent that there was some genetic variation of the capacity to respond in this manner. If selection favoured the response, the frequency with which it occurred increased from generation to

90

generation, until after some time it became practically universal when the selected stock was submitted to the ether. After some time a new gene mutation occurred; this was a sex-linked factor which had not been present in the original stock. Its effect is that females homozygous for it lay eggs which tend to develop the bithorax phenotype. This is particularly striking when the factor is present in the selected stock, in which the bithorax modification has been set on a hair trigger. If, by various types of crossbreeding, the factor is removed from this stock and transferred into an unselected wild type stock, the tendency to produce bithoraxes is very much reduced, though it remains large enough to make it clear that the factor could not have been present in the strain with which the experiment started. We have here an example in which selection has built up a genotype which exhibits a particular type of developmental instability. A gene mutation has occurred which in normal Drosophila would have only a very slight tendency to produce this phenotype but which does so with considerable frequency in the selected stock. Thus, if one merely refers to such a gene mutation as 'random' one does not say by any means everything of interest which can be told about it.

The other main evolutionary effect of the epigenetic system involves a reconsideration of the doctrine concerning the inheritance of acquired characters. It is well known that the development of organisms is usually to some extent canalized, in the sense that even though it may become somewhat modified in response to an environmental stress, it also exhibits a tendency to reach its normal end result in spite of disturbing circumstances. This combination of flexibility and resistance to change can have important evolutionary consequences. If a strain of animals is selected over many generations for its capacity to respond in a particular way to a certain stress, a set of genotypes will, as we have seen, gradually be built up in which this response is easily exhibited when the environmental stress is applied. This is an exhibition of developmental flexibility. If, now, the environmental stress is removed from later generations, and the strain put back into the original conditions, the development of the individuals composing it may still be flexible enough for them to lose some of the specific response, but the developmental resistance to change may be sufficient to ensure that some of it is still retained. If that happens, we should find that a character which at the beginning of the experiment appeared only as a response to a specific environmental stress is now exhibited, in a strain which has been modified by selection, even when the stress is absent. We should have a system which exactly mimics the in-

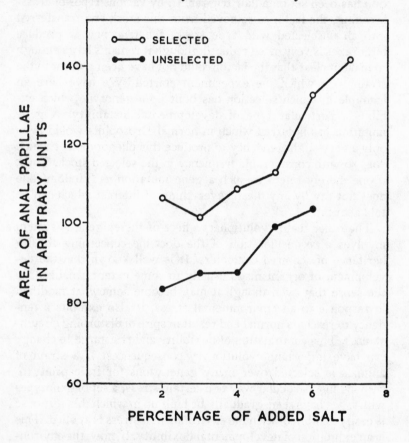

FIG. 1

Graphs showing the area of the anal papillae (related to the total body size) when a selected and a comparable unselected strain of *Drosophila melanogaster* were grown on medium to which various percentages of salt had been added.

heritance of an acquired character, but one which depends not on the direct induction of a hereditary variation, in the manner suggested by Lamarck, but on selection operating on the genetical structure of the population.

Again, there is practical chapter and verse for such a suggestion in the experiments with the bithorax modification mentioned above. After rather more than twenty generations of selection for ease of response to ether vapour, the strain had reached a condition in which a high proportion of bithorax individuals appeared even when the ether treatment was not given.

Perhaps a rather more appealing example is an experiment which has only just been completed.[1] A population of wild type Drosophila was grown on a normal medium to which sufficient sodium chloride had been added to cause the death of the majority of the larvae. As generation succeeded generation under this stringent natural selection, the percentage of survivors gradually increased but the concentration of salt was then also raised so as to maintain the pressure. The osmotic regulation of the Drosophila larva is known to involve a pair of papillae on either side of the anus. After twenty-one generations, flies from three strains which had been submitted to this selection were grown in various concentrations of salt, and the size of their anal papillae compared with that of the initial strains, on which no selection had been exerted. (Fig. 1.)

The figures show, in the first place, that the selection had increased the capacity of the individuals to respond to the stress of the salt. The curve relating the size of the anal organ to the salt content of the medium is steeper in the selected strains than in the unselected. We may say that the selection has improved the adaptability. Secondly, at any particular concentration of salt the size of the anal organ is larger in the selected strain than in the corresponding unselected one. Although under selection the development has become more flexible it still is not flexible enough to allow the selected strains to regress completely to the unselected level when the environmental stress is removed.

We have here a good example of the limitations of a phraseology which attempts to call a character either an acquired one

[1] C. H. Waddington, 1959.

or an inherited one. In reality all characters are both acquired and inherited. But we see also how after selection the genetic system in a population may determine a phenotypic appearance which previously could only be obtained under the combined influence of the initial genotype and a specific environmental stress. This is the process which I have spoken of as the genetic assimilation of an acquired character. Although its mechanism is quite different from the Lamarckian inheritance of acquired characters, being entirely based on the concepts of orthodox Mendelian genetics, it can in fact play in evolutionary theory the very role for which Lamarckian hypotheses have often been invoked.

To obtain a complete picture of the evolutionary system, we need to take into account one further set of factors. These may be spoken of as the 'exploitive system'. Animals are usually surrounded by a much wider range of environmental conditions than they are willing to inhabit. They live in a highly heterogeneous 'ambiance', from which they themselves select the particular habitat in which their life will be passed. Moreover, not only do animals exhibit behaviour which can be considered as the exercise of choice between alternative environments but in many cases they perform actions which modify the environment as it is originally offered to them; for instance, by building nests, burrows, etc. Thus, the animal by its behaviour contributes in a most important way to determining the nature and intensity of the selective pressures which will be exerted on it. Natural selection is very far from being as external a force as the conventional picture might lead one at first sight to believe. Clearly, a whole series of problems arise in this field, but they have as yet been rather little studied, and an understanding of the mutual dependence of selection and behaviour is still largely a matter for the future.

Biological evolution, then, is carried out by an 'evolutionary system' which involves four major factors (Fig. 2): a genetic system, which engenders new variation by the process of mutation and transmits it by chromosomal genes; an epigenetic system, which translates the information in the fertilized egg and that which impinges on it from the environment into the characters of the reproducing adult; an exploitive system, by

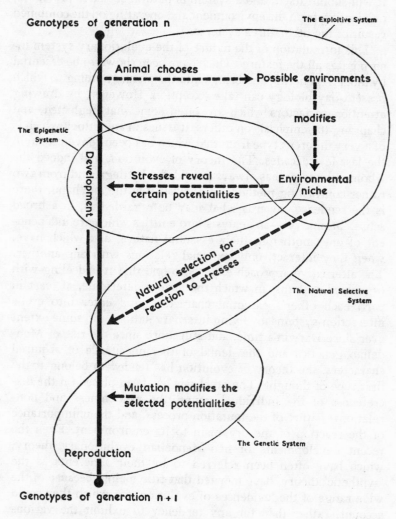

FIG. 2

A diagram of the evolutionary system, showing the four component sub-systems and their inter-relations.

which an animal chooses and modifies the environment to which it will submit itself; and a system of natural selective pressures, originating from the environment and operating on the combined result of the other three systems.

This formulation of the nature of the evolutionary system incorporates all the features which have been shown to be essential by modern genetics, and brings into the picture nothing to which present-day biology can take exception. However, by drawing attention to factors which are often somewhat neglected, and changing the emphasis on others, it issues in an outlook which is of a very different type from that which has been conventional in the last few decades. The theory of evolution, and indeed the whole of biology, has always provided a battleground from two rather contrasting methods of analysis. On the one hand, there is the tendency towards what may be regarded as, in a broad sense, 'atomicity'—an analysis into entities which are independent of one another in their essential nature, and which have, when they interact, only external relations with one another. The alternative approach expects to find that it is dealing with organized systems, in which the factors determine, at least in part, each other's essential characters, and enter into cyclic interaction-systems involving internal relations. To some extent ever since Darwin's time, and still more since the rise of Mendelian genetics and the denial of the inheritance of acquired characters, the theory of evolution has tended to belong to the first type of thought. The emphasis has been placed on the discreteness of the individual genes, the randomness and non-relational nature of the mutation process, and the unimportance of the reaction of the organism to its environment. Even the recent developments of neo-Mendelian evolutionary theory, which have often been referred to by their adherents as the 'synthetic' theory, have merited that title mainly because of the wide range of the 'evidences of evolution' for which they could account, rather than for any tendency to exhibit the various factors involved in the evolutionary process as aspects of a unified general system.

In a recent lecture, the anthropologist Kluckhohn tried to formulate some of the most important alternative types of philosophical outlook which underlie the value systems of various peoples. As his first and most basic pair he took the distinction between a 'determinate' and an 'indeterminate' picture of the world. 'This contrast,' he writes, 'hinges upon the priority given to orderliness (lawfulness) in the universe as opposed to chance or caprice or any factor or factors that make prediction or control impossible *in principle* . . . (it) is between a state of affairs conceived as operating in consistent and lawful fashion and one where an indeterminism (of whatever sort) reigns.' Recent evolution theory has been not only very 'atomistic' but very 'indeterminate' in this sense.

In the exposition of evolutionary mechanisms given here it is not, of course, denied that chance plays a part, particularly in mutation; but these random events are seen as only a part of a complete picture which also includes many forms of cyclic reaction-chains and essential inter-relationships between the constituent elements. The nature of the animal affects the nature of its environment, as well as vice versa; the type of environmental pressure under which the population has been living affects the type of phenotypic modification which mutation is likely to produce; and acquired characters may without too much difficulty become converted into inherited ones by the agency of selection. This way of looking at the situation lays less stress on the atomicity of the various factors, and is also more 'determinate' in Kluckhohn's sense.

Different groups of men may, as Kluckhohn shows, come to attribute value to phenomena because they seem to be determinate, or in other societies, because they are thought to be indeterminate. The kind of value which can be discovered in the two alternative cases will of course differ profoundly. If one has a theory of indeterminate type about some aspects of the world, while the theories about the rest of the world are determinate, the values derived from the two types of outlook may be more or less incompatible with one another. Something of this kind has probably occurred in relation to the theory of evolution in the recent history of our civilization. Most of our values are appropriate to determinate theories. Atomic theories of physics and chemistry impinge on ordinary human life too little to have much influence on our value systems; but when confronted with a theory of biological evolution which emphasizes the atomistic self-sufficiency of the fundamental units, and the importance of chance, many people have not only declined to take very seriously the values (such as novelty, unexpectedness, the opposite of 'getting into a rut', for instance) which might have been found in it, but have either come to the conclusion that the theory amounted to a powerful attack on the 'determinate-type' values which they had previously held, or fallen back on to the defence that the indeterminate theories are in fact 'non-moral' and imply no values of any kind.

A very clear exposition of the points at issue was made recently by the anthropologist and psychiatrist Gregory Bateson; and this gains added interest from the fact that its author is the son of the geneticist William Bateson who had, by his introduction of Mendelism and rejection of the inheritance of acquired characters, perhaps a greater responsibility than anyone else in the English-speaking world for the atomization of evolutionary theory. It is worth quoting this discussion at some length.[1] 'The battle between Darwin and Samuel Butler may have owed some of its bitterness to what looked like personal affronts, but behind all this the argument concerned a question which had religious status. The battle was really about "vitalism". It was a question of how much *life* and what order of life could be assigned to organisms; and Darwin's victory amounted to this, that while he had not succeeded in detracting from the mysterious liveliness of the individual organism, he had at least demonstrated that the evolutionary picture could be reduced to natural "law".

'It was therefore very important to demonstrate that the as yet unconquered territory—the life of the individual organism—could not contain anything which would recapture this evolutionary territory. It was still mysterious that living organisms could achieve adaptive change during their individual lives, and at all costs these adaptive changes, the famous acquired characteristics, must not have influence upon the evolutionary tree. The "inheritance of acquired characteristics" threatened always to recapture the field of evolution for the vitalist side.

[1] 1959.

'. . . Is the battle between non-moral materialism and the more mystical view of the universe affected by a change in the function assigned to the "acquired characteristics"?[2] Does the Newtonian thesis really depend upon the premise that contexts are isolable? Or is our view of the world changed when we admit an infinite regress of contexts, linked to each other in a complex network of meta-relations?

'. . . In breaking away from the Newtonian premise that contexts are always conceptually isolable, I have let in the notion of a universe much more unified—and in that sense more mystical—than the conventional universe of non-moral materialism. Does the new position so achieved give us new grounds for hope that science might answer moral or aesthetic questions?

'I believe that the position is significantly changed. . . .'

These passages bring out very forcefully some of the philosophical implications that have been at issue in the discussion of the mechanism of evolution ever since Darwin's day. I agree entirely with Bateson that the type of thinking which he employs in psychiatric and sociological contexts, and which I suggest is called for in evolution theory—that is, thinking in terms of organized systems, based on cybernetic or feedback interrelations, rather than in terms of isolatable causes and effects—does involve an important alteration in our general picture of the nature of the world which we are trying to understand. However, I should not express this change in quite the way that he does. In the first place, in my opinion the introduction of such concepts as 'vitalism', or even 'life', as explanatory principles can only result in confusion. The influence which I assign to acquired characters on the course of evolution certainly does not invoke processes which are any more 'vitalistic' than those appealed to by conventional selection genetics. The contrast is not so much between mechanism and vitalism, but rather between mechanism and organicism. Or possibly one could even use the Marxist terms, mechanical materialism and dialectical materialism. The view which I am urging, and I think that which Bateson is putting forward, is much more in tune with the thought of

---

[2] Bateson is here referring specifically to my work on 'genetic assimilation', which he discussed at some length earlier in his lecture.

Whitehead than with that of Driesch or Bergson.

Further, the relation between the organicism-mechanism contrast and the moral-non-moral one is probably not as simple as Bateson seems to imply. The processes of evolution in the sub-human world do not, I feel, have of their own nature any ethical quality whatever. And that remains so whether we envisage them in organismic or mechanismic or atomistic or any other terms. It is only man who becomes an 'ethicizing' being, and 'goes in for ethics'. Now certainly once he has become such a being he may attach ethical value to various things in his surroundings; but these values arise within mankind and are only secondarily attributed to non-human entities or processes. Thus if we come to the conclusion that we can reach a fuller understanding of evolution if we view it in terms of organized systems, this does not make any essential difference to the inherent value of the process, since there is none. It would, in theory, be just as easy (or difficult) to attach value to a process of evolution formulated in mechanistic terms as to one expressed in an organismic way.

It is, I suggest, because of certain practical considerations, rather than for theoretical reasons, that an organismic account of evolution seems more congruent with human ethical feelings. Man, I argue, becomes moulded into an ethical being by his interactions with other members of his social group. It might be anticipated, and is in fact generally the case, that he finds great ethical value in co-operation and mutual dependence and considerably less in arbitrariness and self-sufficiency. If, at a later stage in life, he comes to accept the course of evolution as a supra-ethical criterion against which to judge his ethical notions, there will be a strong tendency to transfer ethical feeling to this criterion; and it will probably be easier to do this if the evolutionary process is conceived of in terms of a system of mutually dependent, cybernetically related, factors than it would be if it were formulated mechanistically. The facts of human social life call for organismic values rather than mechanistic ones. It is for this reason that evolution, which in itself has no ethical value, seems easier to bring into relation with our moral feelings when seen organismically than when analysed in a strictly atomistic manner.

CHAPTER 10

The Human Evolutionary System

IT is only when we pass on from the sub-human world to deal with the evolution of man that ethics must, in its own right, enter the picture. In the human species, all the factors of the biological evolutionary system undoubtedly persist: the genetic system, the epigenetic system, the exploitive system, and the natural selective system. But that is not the end of the story. An extremely important advance in theoretical biology was made by Darlington when he discussed in detail what he speaks of as 'the evolution of genetic systems'. In the production of genetic variations, which can be submitted to the action of natural selection, the process of mutation is supplemented by various processes involving the segregation, reassortment and recombination of genetic units. Darlington uses the phrase 'genetic system' to refer to the whole complex of processes by which hereditary variation is brought into being and transmitted, including these processes of recombination as well as those of mutation. He argued that there will be a natural selection in favour of more efficient genetic systems; that is to say, systems which most effectively throw up hereditary variations of the kind that natural selection will favour. The character of the evolutionary mechanism is therefore sufficient to ensure that evolutionary changes will occur in the direction of an increasing efficiency of the genetic system. In this particular respect, therefore, one can see an inevitable and not merely a contingent direction of change.

Quite a large number of radically different genetic systems are now known among biological organisms; perhaps the best discussion of them is by Pontecorvo. Most of them are found among the lower organisms, such as bacteria and fungi. Quite early in evolutionary history a genetic system was brought into being, which involved diploidy in the cells of the body, reduction of the chromosome number during the formation of the gametes, and sexual reproduction. This has proved enormously successful, and little that can be considered a fundamental advance on it has been achieved by any later sub-human organism. Darlington's argument does not, therefore, suffice to define a direction of evolutionary progress which is detailed enough to be useful to us in our present connection, although it is adequate to show that the possibility of discerning such a direction is not to be ruled out on theoretical grounds.

Now, just as the 'genetic system' is subject to evolution, so in broader terms we may say that the whole four-component 'evolutionary system', of which the genetic system is only a part, itself must evolve. The human situation is characterized by an enormously important step in the evolution of the evolutionary mechanism. Indeed, it might be not unreasonable to define humanity by this fact. In man, the processes of teaching by the older members of the population and learning by the younger ones, have been carried to an incomparably higher pitch than is found in any of the prehuman forms of life, where they play only a relatively minor role, for instance, in the determination of bird song, and a few other examples. In man, they have developed not only to highly effective person-to-person learning, as in apprenticeship, but, by the invention of writing and other more recent devices, to an extremely elaborate system by which the whole conceptual understanding of the past is made available to present recruits to human society. We have here what in effect amounts to a new mode of hereditary transmission. It is true that this cannot transmit a new variation in our bodily structure as do the genes, but it can transmit conceptual knowledge, beliefs, feelings, aesthetic creations and other mental phenomena, together with a vast variety of non-human artefacts. It may be referred to as the cultural system.

Within the last few millennia, the human race has acquired capacities which in the non-human world could only have been obtained as the results of evolution. To give a banal example, one may mention the ability to fly. Man has certainly not achieved this capacity by waiting for genes to turn up which have transformed his fore-limbs into wings. In fact there is no evidence that changes in the pool of genes available to the human race had any specific effect on the development of the human conquest of the air. This does not mean, of course, that the genes were irrelevant. Human inventiveness and skill, like any character of any organism, are produced by the interaction of genes with one another and with the environment during development. But so far as one can tell, all the genes necessary to produce men capable of inventing methods of flying had been present in the human population for many generations. What the development of flight was waiting for was not some change in the genetic system, but some change in the cultural system.

When one attempts to consider the problem of human evolution, the type of phenomena which should rise to one's mind as presenting the problem to be discussed are all the most crucial changes which have occurred between, say, the late Stone Age and the present. If one compares the Paleolithic population of scattered nomadic hunters with modern highly populous and complex societies, it is not the comparatively slight changes in bodily structure which differentiate us from Cromagnon man that makes the greatest impression. Human evolution has been in the first place a cultural evolution. Its achievements have been the bringing into being of societies in which contributions deriving from such sources as Magna Carta, Confucius, Newton and Shakespeare can be both perpetuated and utilized.

It is important not to overlook this first impression of what human evolution is all about. It is clear that for an understanding of how the human race has come into the possession of those characteristics which we now think most valuable in human life, a theory is needed which is primarily one of cultural evolution. In man, we have, in addition to the biological evolutionary system, a second one in which the mechanism of social transmission fills the role which in the biological realm falls to genetics, that of passing information from one generation to the next.

It should perhaps be admitted that the idea that there is a characteristically human mode of evolution, based on social transmission of information, and that it is by this novel method that the most important evolutionary changes now occur in the human species, is still not quite generally accepted, although it seems to be gradually gaining adherents. It has, of course, been recognized for a long time that conceptual thought and its social transmission is one of the major defining properties of man, but the view that this provides a basis for a new evolutionary mechanism is of more recent origin.

The concept of human cultural evolution has had a history of rather astonishing vicissitudes. These were recently summarized and discussed by several authors at the Chicago Darwin Centennial Conference.[1] In the years immediately following the appearance of the *Origin of Species*, the science of anthropology was founded by men such as Tyler and Lubbock, who were staunch evolutionists. But the time was not yet come when a coherent story of human evolution could be put together; the best that most of the early anthropologists could do was to emphasize the merits of their own culture as the apex which evolution had reached. By the end of the century, enthusiasm for evolutionary ideas in the study of human culture had almost disappeared (although they were still used, of course, in relation to his anatomy). In fact the notion entered a phase of extreme unpopularity, especially among American social scientists, whose great achievements gave them a dominating position in this subject. As Steward writes: 'One distinguished anthropologist remarked that it (cultural evolution) had the value of "illustrating every known fallacy of logic".' In 1923, the late Ruth Benedict wrote: 'It's dead.'[2] Indeed, the fact that Engels incorporated the evolutionary theories of L. H. Morgan in Marxist doctrine was at one time sufficient grounds to render any American believer in cultural evolution open to suspicion of political subversion.

During this period of eclipse, the idea of cultural evolution retained always a few supporters. Perhaps the most important, in the Western world, was Gordon Childe, an avowed Marxist and a student of human evolution whose learning and acumen could not be disputed. In America, Leslie A. White proclaimed his belief in the applicability of evolutionary ideas to culture, but

[1] In particular, A. Irving Hallowell, A. L. Kroeber and J. H. Steward.
[2] Mead. 1959, p. 57

developed theories concerning a unilinear trend which this evolution must follow which tended to isolate his thought from the general current. The majority of students of cultural affairs turned their attention to topics which a biologist would be tempted to compare with anatomy and physiology rather than to genetics and evolution.

The revival of interest in human cultural evolution was, probably, brought about from outside the professional anthropological field; in fact, by biologists who noticed the potential importance of man's socio-genetic mechanism of passing formation down the generations. Julian Huxley began to draw attention to this as early as 1929,[1] but the point was only very gradually taken up. It was clearly implied in my article of 1941, and I gave a fairly extended, though popular, discussion of it in 1946, but Huxley[2] still had to say that this was by one 'of the few professional biologists who have tried to see . . . the evolutionary implications of human social organization'. Others sympathetic to the idea at that time were Sinnott and Needham.

Even in quite recent times, however, several of the most profound students of biological evolution have discussed the human situation without referring to the possibility that the human method of transmitting information may give rise to a new evolutionary system. For instance, Muller's stimulating papers are concerned almost entirely with the natural selection of genes which control tendencies to various types of behaviour; and Darlington[3] argues that culture is determined by genes and discounts the possibility that it represents a superposed system with a powerful influence of its own. In the recent general symposium on 'Behaviour and Evolution'[4] only Huxley and Margaret Mead show any appreciation of the importance of the novel human evolutionary system. But the point is, perhaps, gradually getting across. For instance, Dobzhansky, who is perhaps the most distinguished evolutionist of today, fully accepts it; in his book *The Biological Basis of Human Freedom* he writes: 'The appearance

---

[1] In Wells, Huxley and Wells.
[2] 1947, p. 185.
[3] 1953.
[4] Ed. Roe and Simpson, 1958.

of culture signified the beginning of a hitherto non-existent type of evolutionary development—the evolution of culture or human evolution proper. . . . Biological heredity is transmitted by genes; consequently it is handed down exclusively from parents to their children and other direct descendants. Culture is transmitted by teaching and learning. At least in principle, 'the social legacy' can be transmitted by anyone to anyone, regardless of biological descent. Man may be said to have two heredities, a biological one and a cultural one; all other organisms have only the biological one' (pp. 26, 27). Another writer trained in the classical doctrines of genetics, Kenneth Mather, has recently expressed the same ideas as follows: 'Ideas have many of the properties which we find in genes . . . they are transmissible, and therefore permanent in the same sense as genes, they vary and they are selected. Because they vary and are selected, the caucus of ideas and concepts on which the structure of society depends is not only capable of evolution but must in fact evolve. . . . This social evolution . . . has come to overlay and obscure the genetical variation which we see when we look within societies.' Thus the view that I have been putting forward, that the cultural or 'socio-genetic' system provides a basic mechanism on which a new type of evolutionary system can operate, is certainly not without extremely weighty support from biologists.

In the meantime, anthropologists have also become better disposed towards it. Although Kroeber reports that when Huxley first stressed the importance of cultural evolutionary processes to a group of anthropologists at the Wenner-Gren Foundation in 1952, he aroused mainly unrest and opposition, he goes on: 'I do not know precisely why.' However, in 1955, Huxley was invited to contribute a guest editorial to the *Yearbook of Anthropology*, and by the time the Chicago and Edinburgh Darwin Centennial Conferences took place this year, many anthropologists were claiming to be evolutionists. In some cases, however, it is not very clear how this differs from a statement that they are becoming interested in the history of cultures. The distinction most anthropologists seem to have in mind is, perhaps, best drawn by Steward, who writes: 'Two essential features, however, distinguish cultural evolution from the cultural historical approach. First, cultural evolution seeks internal causes or processes as the explanation of change rather than the external process of diffusion. . . . Second, cultural evolution ascribes primary importance to structures that differ qualitatively from their antecedents, and it therefore bases taxonomy upon stages rather than areas.' Other points on which Steward lays stress are the acceptance of a multi-linearity of cultural evolution, and of the importance of the external environment in influencing its course.

Of the two 'essential features', the second is clearly related to the formulation of an evolutionary taxonomy of cultures, while the first is, as it stands, little more than the assertion that evolution occurs. Few anthropologists have in fact succeeded in throwing fresh light on their subject by using the concepts with which biological evolutionists work—that is, transmission of information down the generations, and the limitation of this information by selective agencies. Perhaps the outstanding exception is Margaret Mead, whose interest in the mechanism of cultural transmission through the generations by parent-child contact has brought her into direct relation with problems which are formally similar to those which fall in the province of genetics in the non-cultural field.

The most important task, for anthropologists anxious to increase our insight into the processes of cultural evolution, would seem to be the detailed study of the various components of the socio-genetic system as they operate in mankind today. Probably a great many relevant data already exist in the literature, but it is clearly out of the question for a biologist to attempt to dig them out or evaluate them. However, it is possibly of some interest to try to formulate the sort of questions which arise in the mind of one who turns from the study of the biological evolutionary mechanism to reflect on the evolutionary situation of man.

In the first place, the existence of a human cultural evolutionary mechanism does not, of course, imply that the biological evolutionary mechanism has ceased to operate in man. Although it would seem prudent when faced by a phenomenon of human evolution, first to consider by what cultural means it has been brought about, it is also very necessary to enquire into the biological or genetical phenomena associated with it. This is, however, exceedingly difficult. What we should like to do is to discover how closely the operations of the cultural and the biological evolutionary systems are linked together. Suppose a marked change takes place in the gene pool of the human population; under what circumstances should we expect this to have an important influence on the essential cultural achievements of the group concerned? It is extraordinarily difficult to find any factual evidence, since most examples of marked changes in the gene pool of a population involve the immigration or emigration of individuals who carry with them not only their transmissible genes but also their transmissible culture. For instance, one may postulate, as Darlington has done, that the emigrants from Ireland in the middle of the last century carried out of the population many genes for various types of socially effective behaviour, leaving the home population impoverished. But in practice the existence of these genes is only hypothetical, and even if they did exist the emigrants carried with them, also and undoubtedly, culturally transmitted tendencies to vigorous behaviour. Similarly the argument popular in many American circles that the immigrants brought with them genetically determined capacities for hard work and enterprise fails to distinguish these from culturally transmitted tendencies of the same kind.

There are a few cases, however—for instance, when Jewish populations have immigrated into or out of a country with whose population they have not engaged in extensive cross-breeding but on whose life they have exerted a considerable influence—in which one may deduce that this influence has been primarily a cultural rather than a genetic one. Even if we were to make the unsafe assumption that, for instance, it is their genes which endow the Jewish people or the Chinese with great ability in trade, the effect which a small number of Jews or Chinese may have on the economic existence of the people surrounding them can only be the result of cultural rather than genetic transmission. Again, the rapidity, in terms of numbers of generations, with which many steps of evolution take place (such as, say, the formation of the characteristic United States culture out of an extraordinarily mixed European immigrant population) is hardly compatible with the operations of the genetic evolutionary mechanism and, it would seem, must in the main be attributed to the actions of the human cultural evolutionary system.

The obvious counterpart to the question of what cultural effects are to be expected when a genetic change takes place in a human population, is the problem of whether, when we can discern cultural differences between two human groups, the main responsibility of these may be expected to lie with the system of cultural transmission or with that of genetic transmission. Again, from an *a priori* standpoint one must expect differences in both systems to be involved, but it is exceedingly difficult to find evidence which allows us incontrovertibly to assess the relative importances of the two contributing factors. It is quite clear that races such as the West Africans, the Maoris and the Chinese differ genetically from Europeans. Some of these genetic differences are obviously expressed in skin colour; there must surely be others more difficult to detect. But have we any reason whatever to suppose that the genetic differences, whatever they may be, have played a critical role in determining those distinctions between these human groups which we would consider important in the grand picture of human evolution as a whole? Is there any reason, for instance, to suppose that it is the differences in the gene pool between the Chinese and the European populations which have caused the one to develop a social system based on such relatively unindividualistic systems as Confucianism and Buddhism and the other a civilization inspired by such a different system of thought and feeling as Christianity? I see no *a priori* to suppose anything of the kind; nor is there sufficient factual evidence to establish such a conclusion.

Again, one can find examples, particularly in quite recent times, in which human populations have changed in such respects in periods of time which seem much too short to allow of noteworthy alterations in their genetic endowment. Such a change is in fact probably proceeding in China at this moment. The change in West Africa, from the conditions described a century ago to the present situation of highly sophisticated and technologically competent modern societies, can only have been accompanied by exceedingly small, if any, changes in the general gene pool. One of the most striking of such changes, and one of the very few that has been carefully studied by a highly trained specialist, is that of the Manus people of the Admiralty Islands in the Pacific studied by Margaret Mead.[1] This transformation from a palaeolithic to at least the beginnings of a modern society has taken place within a lifetime, that is to say, it has involved *no* genetic alteration. It is a most remarkable example of how powerful the cultural evolutionary system may be. However, the details of the situation bring out rather clearly just what the importance of genetic factors may be in such instances of cultural evolution. Mead shows that the change in Manus culture was focused around one, or very few, unusual individuals, without whose special qualities it would probably not have occurred—as indeed it did not occur, to anything like the same degree, in a number of neighbouring cultures. The extraordinary abilities of the main leader of the 'Manus revolution' would seem likely to be, in the main, the result of a fortunate genetic constitution. If this is so, genetic potentialities were in fact important in influencing the course of change. But the crucial points are, firstly, that the population in that region of the world possessed genetic resources such that unusually able individuals are produced from time to time in one or other of the small cultural groups: and secondly, that the general population was culturally transformed with being simultaneously genetically altered.

These examples suggest, in my opinion, that in producing the changes of the kind which we consider of major importance in the evolution of mankind, the cultural system of transmission is usually contributing incomparably more than the genetical. Even when we can be certain that genetical changes have occurred, as for instance in the comparison between Africans and Europeans, there are only one or two examples in which these changes can be shown to have any practical importance. An example may be the high frequency of the sickle cell gene in certain African populations. But the great majority of the definitely proven genetical changes relate to such matters as skin colour and hair form, which are entirely trivial in the perspective of man's progress since palaeolithic era. Where cultural changes have occurred, however, as in the Manus or the immigrant population

[1] 1956.

into the United States, the real importance of the evolutionary alterations is unquestionable.

The evidence which, to my mind, is the most convincing in leading one to lay more stress on the cultural than on the genetical mechanism of human evolution, is the speed at which the changes have occurred. This is often, as I have argued above, much too great to be reconcilable with a genetic mechanism, but even when it is not, one should remember that one ought to expect in the cultural evolutionary system some phenomena comparable to what is known as genetic homeostasis in the biological mechanism of evolutionary change. The genetic system of a population, as Lerner in particular has pointed out, shows a considerable power of resistance to factors such as natural or artificial selection which attempt to alter it. I have argued that the epigenetic system shows similar characteristics of unresponsiveness. One might expect, and I think the evidence suggests, that cultural systems also have some tendency to stability. This is probably correlated to some extent with their size. The fantastically rapid transformation of Manus society occurred in a minute population of only a few thousands; one could hardly expect the fifty millions of Nigeria or the five hundred millions of China to alter as rapidly. One cannot, therefore, always expect the processes of change mediated by the cultural evolutionary system to occur in a shorter time than those which might be carried out by the genetic system. It is only in favourable cases that the critical evidence emerges which shows that steps in human evolution can take place at a rate much faster than the genetic mechanisms could bring about. Cultural phenomena which involve stability over long periods, such as the persistence of the caste system in India or the characteristics of Northern as contrasted with Mediterranean civilization in Europe, need not necessarily, on *a priori* grounds, be attributed to the genetical system; there is no reason to doubt that cultural transmission may operate over many generations. Such questions will only be answerable when we find further methods of gathering empirical data which will enable us to distinguish the contributions of the two information-transmitting systems in each particular case.

Let us consider next the various factors which make up the

biological evolutionary system, and see what parallels we can find for them in the specifically human evolutionary system. In biological evolution transmission of information from one generation to the next is in the main carried out by the genetic system. In this the transmitting event occurs at the time of fertilization, when each parent contributes to the newly-formed individual a set of hereditary units or genes. These units are essentially quite separate from one another, but in practice they are usually associated together in groups, and that in two different ways. As far as the biological genetic system is concerned, the most relevant form of association is a quite contingent one, which depends on the fact that the genes are located on chromosomes. Their arrangement into groups of neighbours held together by the material structure of the chromosome is usually, though not always, more or less irrelevant to their functioning. Another type of association between genes arises during development. The formation of the different tissues of the body, such as muscle, nerve, etc., depends on the inter-related functioning of sets of genes. In a certain sense, therefore, each specialized tissue of the body represents the activities of a group of genes (or perhaps better, represents a group of gene activities), the association of the members of the group being in this case not at all a matter of chance, since it is essentially dependent on the way in which the gene activities interlock and interact with one another.

These epigenetic groupings of genes—that is to say, groupings which arise from their activities during development—are not reflected in the normal transmission of information between generations of animals by the genetic mechanism. It is relevant to the human situation, however, to remember that even in animals something more may be involved between generations than the standard genetic system concerned with nuclear genes. The mother always contributes to the new animal a relatively massive amount of egg cytoplasm. In some groups of animals, for instance in insects, during the maturation of the egg in the maternal ovary a large amount of the contents of certain other cells, known as nurse cells, is bodily injected into the developing egg. These nurse cells could be taken to represent one particular epigenetic grouping of gene activities, which thus becomes to some extent transmitted to the next generation. Again, in many animals which bear their young alive there are formed, by developmental processes in the mother, mechanisms for passing into the offspring certain of the results of the activities of epigenetic gene-groupings in her body. For instance, substances from the maternal blood may be passed into the offspring through a placenta or similar structure. The most striking of such developments in the animal world is, of course, the development of milk secretion in mammals. We know several clear-cut examples in which transmission through such 'para-genetic mechanisms', as they might be called, can be shown to produce easily demonstrable effects on the offspring. Typical examples are the milk factor concerned with tumour development in mice, and the effects of the maternal body-size on the growth of the young embryo in reciprocal egg-transplantations between mammals of different sizes. In the sub-human world, however, the para-genetic mechanisms which can be utilized for transmitting to the next generation the results of the epigenetic interactions between genes are only rather slightly developed.

The situation is very different in the specifically human evolutionary system. The cultural, or as we may call it, the 'socio-genetic', transmission mechanism does not operate entirely or even mainly at one point in the life history of the new generation. There is no single entity that has to carry the message from one generation to the next as the gametes do in the biological world. We have, as it were, an enormous expansion and multiplication of modes of para-genetic transmission. An individual can receive information from his forebears hroughout the whole, or at least the greater part of life, although, as we know only too well, the task of getting new ideas through his skull becomes progressively harder after a certain age.

This escape from the domination of a single major transmitter such as the gamete makes it possible for the socio-genetic system to handle groups of units which are associated, not only by chance as are the linkage groups of genes on the chromosomes, but which are grouped together by their functional interactions, in a manner comparable to the organized groups of gene activities which arise during development.

If one were to attempt, therefore, to break down the content of social transmission into a series of unit items one should expect to find these items associated into groups in two different ways. It is easy to recognize one of them in the functional interrelations between different items of transmitted content; the varied elements involved in a complex industrial technique, or the inter-related beliefs comprising one particular church doctrine, would provide examples. It is clear that the socio-genetic mechanism is quite capable of handing on such organized groups of units, the organization being a functional one and comparable to that which characterizes the tissues of an animal's body; that is, it is of a kind which in general is not capable of biological transmission to the next generation.

But we might ask if there are also chance associations which could be regarded as comparable to the linkage between genes which happen to lie on the same chromosome. For instance, in the transmission of western culture to oriental nations it is very common to find that an item such as the wearing of western dress tends to be associated with other items such as various industrial techniques, or belief in the dogmas of Christianity. There is clearly very little essential functional connection between industrialism and the wearing of trousers rather than a sarong, dhoti or kimono. The association between such items, in so far as it exists, would seem to be a purely contingent one, quite comparable to that between different genes in a single linkage group. Social anthropology seems in recent years to have been so interested in establishing the reality of the functional connections between elements of culture that the possible importance of purely fortuitous associations, comparable to those of linked genes, has perhaps been somewhat neglected.

As a matter of fact sub-human evolution has involved not only the true genetic mechanism, and the para-genetic mechanisms such as transmissions through mammary secretions. There is a further subtlety, which is concerned with questions which almost merit the name of 'metagenetics'. As Darlington in particular has emphasized, any particular mode of genetic transmission,

for instance one depending on chromosomes and bisexual reproduction with cross fertilization, endows the organisms which
utilize it with certain capacities for evolutionary modification.
Another mode of genetic transmission, for instance one in which
the organisms are self-fertilizing hermaphrodites, carries with it
different capabilities for performing evolutionary advance. During the existence of living things on earth there have been,
Darlington claims, alterations in these modes of genetic operation; there has been an 'evolution of genetic systems', as he
terms it. The most important steps in this have been the organization of genes into chromosomes, the adoption of bisexual reproduction, and of course the evolution of the socio-genetic
mechanism. Once it has appeared, we can find a parallel process,
which is an 'evolution of socio-genetic mechanisms'. In particular, there has been a development of phenomena of the kind
which Bateson has called deutero-learning, that is to say, learning to learn. In this, the content which is acquired from the
learning process is the ability to learn other things more quickly
or more efficiently. This is an example of a second order improvement in the mechanism of social transmission, comparable
to the improvements (from the point of view of evolution) in
the genetic system discussed by Darlington.

The development of deutero-learning introduces concepts
which we might consider 'meta-socio-genetical'. There have,
however, also been many evolutionary advances of a less radical
nature in the socio-genetic system. They have produced alterations, which from the point of view of human evolution can in
the main be considered as improvements, in the mechanisms of
social transmission. Some of them have recently been discussed
by Mead.[1] There is, for instance, a very primitive kind of social
transmission of experience, which in fact many animals other
than man also exhibit. In this, transmission occurs direct from
individual to individual, through unverbalized behaviour of the
teacher which conveys some inarticulate message to the learner,
either as a model to be imitated or as a directive to some course
of action. This primitive mode of transmission often persists as
an accompaniment to the more highly evolved socio-genetic

[1] 1958.

mechanisms. Posture, gesture, turn of phrase, stress and accent all convey whatever it is they do convey in this manner. Although it is primitive and undifferentiated, this mode of transmission is not without power. The characteristics which differentiate the products of the best public schools and Oxbridge from those of the secondary modern and Red Brick have been in the main passed over by this mechanism which man shares with such other social creatures as the red deer and the prairie dog.

The main defect of this model-mimic or leader-follower system of transmission is its relative inefficiency in handling items of information which are capable of being conceptualized. It can indeed transmit emotional or affective material which is by no means simple, but there is a great deal of human experience for which other systems of socio-genetic transmission have, it appears, proved much more efficient. The simplest of these systems can indeed be regarded as only a formalization and extension of the inarticulate model-mimic arrangement. This is the apprenticeship system, in which teaching is still largely by showing and only partially in the form of words and formal instructions. Human apprentice teaching, however, differs from animal model-mimic transmission in such factors as the conscious utilization of repetition as a means of indoctrination, and in its development of a long-term course of instruction leading towards a definite recognized goal. It is still utilized even in the most highly evolved societies at many levels of sophistication, from the training of a plumber or cobbler through that of a doctor or lawyer to the most rarefied spiritual level of a guru and his pupil.

The next step in the evolution of socio-genetic transmission mechanisms is, perhaps, the formalization of rote learning. In general, in modern societies rote learning is used to inculcate information which has somewhere or other been recorded in written form. This is the case, for instance, in the rote learning of the Koran or the Confucian classics which are features of classical Mohammedan and Chinese education. The existence of a written text is, however, not a necessary adjunct of rote learning. One might hazard the guess, for instance, that the bards of Homer's day, like the court singers of classical Ireland,

Iceland and West Africa, to name a few cultures at random, were taught largely by rote with an almost total absence of any writing.

It was, of course, the invention of writing which removed from the socio-genetic mechanism the necessity for person-to-person contact between the transmitter and the recipient. It is scarcely necessary, and certainly impractical in a context such as this, to elaborate the steps in the development of techniques of social transmission through recorded conceptual language. I will only make the remark—not entirely a facetious one—that impressive though these advances have been in some respects, we seem in some ways only too reluctant to take advantage of them. Why, the university teacher often thinks, must he continue to spend so much of his time using for the nth year in succession a technique of instruction which was sensible enough for his forefathers who had no alternative method available except manuscript treatises inscribed on vellum? Whereas, he nowadays could so easily record, not only his voice, but if you wish an accurate representation of his expression and gestures, on a piece of magnetic tape, while he himself wrote learned works in a villa in the south of France or conducted experiments in his laboratory.

It is characteristic of all the more highly evolved means of socio-genetic transmission that they do not depend essentially on person-to-person contact. The biological genetic system has of course never escaped this limitation. Every individual animal must have an individual mother and the majority of them an individual father also. The major weakness of the biological system from an evolutionary point of view is that, although it ensures some mixing of hereditary qualities from different individuals, it limits the number of individuals which can participate in this mixing to only two; and in practice it usually operates to reduce the difference between these two since it is difficult to persuade a mother and father of widely different kinds to hybridize. This restriction on hybridization is very greatly reduced in the human socio-genetic system.

One of the major features of human evolutionary processes, in fact, is the incorporation into one culture of elements which

117

have arisen in another. The process is comparable to what is known in the botanical world as introgressive hybridization. In the biological realm the results from a wide hybridization usually differ from one another not so much by the presence or absence of individual genes, but rather by the persistence or loss from the strain of whole chromosomes. In the socio-genetic system of man also, when cultures come in contact it seems that what they take from each other is not a number of separate discrete items, but rather large portmanteau chunks of information. It is not, I think, quite clear whether these chunks are comparable to chromosomes; that is to say, are composed of a more or less randomly-associated set of items which happen to occur together, as do the genes in a linkage group on the chromosome, or whether the chunks are always more highly organized in a manner comparable to the epigenetically-interactive groups of gene activities which characterize the different tissues of an animal body. When one culture adopts from another, say, a religion such as Christianity, it is clear that we are dealing with a group of items which is organized and which is comparable rather to an epigenetic grouping then to a purely genetic linkage group. On the other hand, when the Indian culture adopts from the British such diverse items as a taste for cricket, a particular method of parliamentary election, a certain organization of the army, and a special administrative jargon such as 'I beg you to do the needful', it seems rather more likely that we are dealing with the introgression of an arbitrarily associated group of items, comparable to the genes in a chromosome.

The varied items of information which are transmitted by these different mechanisms must have originated in some way when they first began their social career. It has been suggested above that in the socio-genetic system incorporation of items from other cultures (processes comparable to introgressive hybridization), and the transmission of complexes of units whose unity is essentially epigenetic, are both much more frequent and important processes than the comparable happenings in the sub-human biological system. But they cannot be the whole story of the origin of variation in the human cultural heritage. There must be some process by which new items of socially transmissible information are added to the human store. In biological evolution much of the genetic variation in a population is created anew in each generation by recombination of already existing genes, but we fully realize that this shuffling is essentially a second order process, based on a primary process of mutation by which new alleles are created. What is the comparable process to mutation in the socio-genetic system?

The answer must be twofold. In the first place, one may point out that in socio-genetics a process comparable to the inheritance of acquired characters undoubtedly occurs. Cultural transmission, as we have seen, does not depend on specialized transmitting entities comparable to gametes, but the situation is as though any differentiated tissue of animal's body could transmit its qualities direct to the next generation. Thus, much of the new variation in socio-genetically transmitted items can arise as acquired characters, from the interaction between the human beings in the population and their surroundings. The human evolutionary system can thus utilize a vast source of variation which is more or less closed to the sub-human world. But it is by no means certain that all new socio-genetically transmissible items arise in this way. Man appears to develop ideas whose nature is not a necessary consequence of the environmental circumstances, and in so far as this is the case, these ideas can scarcely arise solely as acquired characters. It is difficult, for instance, to deny that there is some arbitrary element in the distinction between the great religions, such as Christianity and Buddhism. There would seem to be a place in the genesis of new human ideas for some process which shares with gene mutation a characteristic of randomness and unpredictability.

We have recently come to realize that a very important property of the biological genetic system is the existence within natural populations of a tendency which has been called genetic homeostasis. A natural population of animals contains a pool of genes, the particular genetic endowment of any one individual being a sample drawn out of this pool. If some disturbing agency, such as natural selection, is applied to the population, the frequency of the various genes in the pool will be altered. The tendency of the population to genetic homeostasis is exhibited by the fact that when the selection pressure is released the frequencies of the various genes frequently return towards, or even reach, their original values. The genetic make-up of the population, in fact, exhibits some resistance to agents which would tend to change it. A similar balance between a certain degree of flexibility combined with some resistance to modifying agents is, as we have pointed out above, also shown by the epigenetic systems which lead from the egg to the adult condition.

In the socio-genetic system there are parallels for both these types of qualified stability. In human culture, however, it is not so easy to distinguish between them. As we have seen, the socio-genetic system includes phenomena comparable to the inheritance of acquired characteristics and the transmission of epigenetically organized complexes. Thus there are several mechanisms by which a human culture can manifest resistance to change, but it is not easy to classify them in groups comparable to those which are applicable to the biological evolutionary system. One agent opposing change may be the mechanism of socio-genetic transmission itself; for instance, many cultural traits which are conveyed by the primitive inarticulate transmission mechanism, which was discussed first above, seem to be very resistant to change, probably because of the transmission filter through which they have to pass. Examples are the somewhat nebulous, but often easily recognizable, qualities which are often spoken of as national characteristics, such as Jewishness or Indianness. This is perhaps something near to biological genetic homeostasis in its strict sense. At the other end of the range there are tendencies to stability in human culture which arise from what is clearly an epigenetic unity; for instance, a closely organized body of dogmas such as that of the Roman Catholic Church is not at all easy to alter and tends to be transmitted more or less unchanged from generation to generation. In between these two extremes there are very many intergrades. It does not seem likely that much purpose would be served by trying to classify them on the basis of their logical similarity to comparable genetic and epigenetic phenomena in biology.

There is in this general field one consideration about human society which does, I think, raise some interesting questions. Most animals retain only for a very short fraction of their life-span any capacity to be modified by their environment. The period in which they are epigenetically flexible is comparatively short. Man can—indeed in the present century probably must—go on learning throughout practically his whole life. One might then institute a comparison between a whole generation within a given human culture and a single animal individual, regarding the changes which the human generation undergoes during its life-time as comparable to the changes which the egg will undergo as it develops into an adult. One would find then, I think, that what we may call the 'socio-epigenetic' system of a generation varies considerably from culture to culture. In some there is much more resistance to change during a given life-time than in others. In American culture, for instance, it is a matter of pride that an individual should adopt new habits and modes of life as they come along. In Britain, classical China, and many other countries much more value is attached to clinging to the old ways. This is very comparable to the fact that in animal species one can find some whose development is extremely resistant to modification by the environment—is, in fact, what has been called strongly canalized—while in others the epigenetic processes are much more flexible. For instance, mice inhabit a very large variety of habitats, but look very much the same in all of them, whereas some invertebrate species are so easily modifiable that almost every pond in which they live has its own recognizable population. In the biological realm the strength and character of the epigenetic canalization can certainly be controlled by selection, and is a factor which plays an important role in evolution. In the socio-genetic system the readiness to accept change within a generation must also be both influenced by, and itself influence, the evolutionary process.

Closely allied with these matters is the problem which Darwin made central in his work—the problem of speciation. It is an empirical fact that living organisms do not vary continuously over the whole range which they exhibit, but that they fall into more or less well defined groups, which are commonly called

121

species. The precise definition of what constitutes a species is a matter of great difficulty, about which biologists are hardly yet in agreement, but that some significant discontinuity occurs can scarcely be questioned. Paradoxically enough, however, the origin of species is just the facet of evolution on which Darwin's theories throw the feeblest illumination. We still have very little understanding of why discontinuity occurs so frequently. We have to suppose that in some way certain constellations of hereditary potentialities fit together into a stable pattern, while other combinations are inharmonious; but that is only a very abstract and general statement. But, although biologists do not understand it, here is an area of enquiry which, one feels, sociologists will also have to face. To what extent is discontinuity a characteristic of the variation between human cultures?

It is, of course, a fact of the first importance about mankind that the human group has not split into biologically distinct species. There is no other group of higher mammals (except some of man's domesticated animals) which have such a widespread distribution over the surface of the earth without becoming broken up into species which differ from one another in their genetical constitution, though parallels to the human situation could be found in lower types of beings such as some insects, protozoa, etc. That all men are brothers is, however, a well-recognized biological fact, whose importance scarcely needs emphasis here.

It is true, of course, that mankind exhibits some local differentiation. If this is comparatively trivial on the level of the biological genetical system, one may still ask how profound it is in relation to the more fluid socio-genetic system. Do human cultures differ from one another in a manner which it might be illuminating to compare with biological specific differences? To the outsider it would seem that we find phenomena extremely similar to those with which the biologist is familiar; some instances of sharp distinctions between even closely neighbouring cultures, as in such a culturally diversified area as New Guinea; some examples of more or less continuous geographical variation, comparable to the formation of local races, in widespread cultures such as, to take an extreme example, the British with its offshoots in Canada, New Zealand, Australia, etc.; and a similar tendency for the initial slight geographical variants to evolve into fully distinct 'species'. The dynamics of this process —for instance its dependence on, or independence of, the formation of barriers to cross-mating—would appear to present sociologists with problems very similar in their formal structure at least to those with which biologists are wrestling.

Finally, I think the biologist would wish to ask the sociologist whether there is in his system of ideas anything which plays the evolutionary role of natural selection. Something, after all, must decide which new items of culture, either adopted from other societies by processes akin to hybridization or arising 'out of the blue' by some analogue of mutation, will succeed in persisting for many generations. Why, for example, were Christ and Mohammed accepted as Messiahs out of all the candidates for that role? Or why were Lamarck's and, for a long time, Mendel's ideas rejected while Darwin's won immediate acclaim? The processes are, perhaps, so complicated that we cannot hope to find any general portmanteau term like 'Natural Selection' to apply to them. But one wonders whether this is not too pessimistic a view. The natural selective value of a new biological variant depends on the number of its offspring. Is it possible that the ability to persist of a new cultural item could be deduced from the magnitude of its cultural progeny—its ability to 'cross-breed' with already existing facets of the culture and to beget issue from them? And of course we should not forget that many biologists now attribute a considerable influence to the fluctuations of random sampling as a phenomenon which mitigates the rigours of strict natural selection. How great a role does pure chance play in preservation or disappearance of new cultural items?

In making these remarks about human evolution it has not been my intention to suggest that our knowledge about the biological evolutionary system will enable us to answer the problems with which sociologists are confronted. All I have tried to show is that a number of quite interesting lines of thought emerge if one takes in turn each of the factors which we consider important in biological evolution, and asks oneself what corresponds to them in the human cultural system.

In the present context, the most important point to note is that it is of the essential nature of the evolutionary system that it must itself evolve. The argument for this conclusion is essentially similar to that which Darlington employed in pointing to the inevitable evolution of the genetic system. In both the restricted case he considered, and in the more general one I have indicated, we are confronted with systems which are so organized that they must 'learn'—that is to say, they must improve their efficiency of operation. This determinacy, of course, does not necessarily extend to defining the details of the manner in which the improvement is brought about. We may safely conclude that there must be an evolution of evolutionary systems, but it would be hazardous, to say the least, to attempt at present to give reasons why this evolution should have gone in exactly the direction which it has taken in the appearance in the living world of the human species. I shall consider in a later chapter, in somewhat more detail, the very peculiar and in some ways bungling manner in which the progress of the evolutionary system to the human stage has actually been achieved.

CHAPTER 11

The Course of Evolutionary Progress

THE thesis that the evolutionary system is such that it is characterized by an inherent tendency to evolve in the direction of greater efficiency does not of course imply that such progressive improvements always occur in every evolutionary sequence. There may be other tendencies also in operation, and in some cases these may be dominant and prevent the improvement

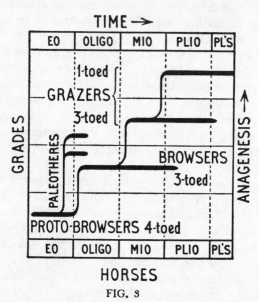

FIG. 3

Diagram of anagenesis and stasigenesis in the evolution of horses during the Tertiary period (Eocene, Oligocene, Miocene, Pliocene and Pleistocene subperiods). Some of the intermediate types of horse persisted (by stasigenesis) for a considerable time before becoming extinct. The Palaeotheres evolved in the same anagenetic direction as the true horses but became extinct at an early period.
(From Huxley 1958.)

either of the evolutionary system as a whole or of one or more of its subsystems.

The actual results which evolution has produced are at present usually considered in terms of three categories. For the sake of clarity it may be as well to introduce the actual technical terms which are employed for these. They have been particularly well discussed in a valuable paper by Julian Huxley.[1]

The three categories are: (1) *Stasigenesis*, the attainment of a biologically satisfactory condition which persists unchanged through long evolutionary periods. Striking examples are provided by such well-known cases as the Brachiopod *Lingula* which seems to have remained almost unaltered since the Ordovician, the recently discovered Coelacanth *Latimeria*, and some other similar isolated and frequently discussed species. However, it must not be forgotten that the persistence of quite large and diversified but primitive groups of animals, such as for instance the Dipnoid fishes or monotremes, are examples on a larger scale of the same category. (2) *Cladogenesis*, the evolution of a diversified range of species and genera all falling within a single basic organizational type. This is of course an absolutely general phenomenon. The appearance of a multiplicity of, for instance, Dipteran flies, or deer, or land snails, are just a few random examples. (3) *Anagenesis*, the appearance of something which can be recognized as an improvement over the previously existing type.

It is the concept of anagenesis which requires the greatest attention in the present context. An example which brings out some of the important points is summarized by Huxley in the diagram reproduced in Fig. 3. This relates to the evolution of the horse family during recent geological periods (Eocene, Oligocene, Miocene, Pliocene and Pleistocene). The evolutionary sequence started with small, four-toed animals which lived by browsing on bushes and low herbage. They evolved in the direction of animals which fed by grazing on grass, and which relied on their fleetness of foot to escape from their enemies. The whole group of animals, considered in relation to the needs of its mode of life, can be considered as falling within a broad

[1] 1958.

general type of biological organization. Within this type of organization, a series of improvements took place during evolution. For instance, the speed of running was improved by the lengthening of the legs, which involved a reduction of the area of the foot which comes in contact with the ground to three and finally to a single toe, the other bones eventually disappearing. Again, the structure and size of the teeth became increased in a way which would improve their efficiency at grinding hard grass during a long lifetime. Changes of this kind are clearly improvements in efficiency as judged by the frame of reference given by the general type of organization. They constitute anagenesis, and Huxley has introduced the very useful word 'grades' to indicate the successive levels through which the improvement has passed. As the diagram indicates, several of the earlier grades of organization, for instance that of three-toed browsers, persisted for quite long periods subsequent to the appearance of some of the higher grades such as the grazers. Such persistence is, in his terminology, stasigenesis. Finally, within each grade diversification into different species and genera occurred. This cladogenesis is not indicated in the diagram (Huxley uses the word 'clades' for groups produced by diversification without change of grade).

A set of grades such as those exemplified in the evolution of the horses falls into a hierarchical order which is defined by— or if you like, itself defines—a general scheme of biological organization characteristic of the group concerned. Now, what is an improvement for a horse may very well be something quite different from a wider point of view. The horse anagenesis has in fact led to a highly specialized creature with only one toe on each foot, highly fitted for carrying out one type of life but quite unable to earn its living in nature except in that specialized manner. If one considers from a long-term point of view the evolution of land-living mammals in general, it becomes apparent that the course which evolution has followed in the horse group has cut it off from the possibility of following some of the lines of change which were potentially open to its remote ancestors, for instance, the development of a manipulative hand. Anagenesis may therefore lead to an evolutionarily dead end.

Huxley recognized that in using the word to cover any improvement within a given type of biological organization he was employing it in a wider sense than had been done by Rensch, who was originally responsible for introducing the words 'anagenesis' and 'cladogenesis'. Rensch[1] used the word for a 'Höherentwicklung' or 'Vervollkommung'. By this he meant an improvement in grade which did not, at least to any marked degree, restrict the potentialities for future evolutionary developments. For instance, the specialization of part of the body surface (either external or internal) for the function of respiratory exchange as in gills or lungs does not carry any obvious limitations with it, and moreover opens up the possibility of utilizing the rest of the surface for other purposes, such as protection or the absorption of digested food materials. Again, the anagenetic improvement of an incipient tendency to become independent of water for supporting the body weight, for respiratory exchange and for the development of the eggs and larva, obviously led to an increase in the possibilities of evolutionary alteration rather than a restriction of them. If we continue, as seems wise, to use anagenesis in the wide sense suggested by Huxley, we can then distinguish two types of anagenetic change: a 'closing' type which leads to improvement within one type of biological organization but a restriction of future potentialities, and an 'opening' type which involves improvement but no noticeable restriction.

It is with this conceptual apparatus that we can now consider the evolution of the evolutionary system and of the sub-systems of which it is composed.

It is probably the natural selective sub-system which we can dispose of most readily, having the least to say about it. There are, of course, several different categories of natural selection. For instance, we may have a natural selection which operates between individuals, which is the type one perhaps most usually considers; but we also have natural selection which acts as between populations. The latter type is very important in some cases, for instance, in animals which live in temporary pools of water which frequently dry up, or in parasites which live in hosts

[1] 1947.

which die and from which they cannot easily escape. It is probably the case that individual natural selection is more important, and population natural selection less, in the more highly evolved animals, a major reason for this being simply that these animals are of large size. Under most circumstances, individual natural selection would probably be more efficient than population selection in producing evolutionary change, and it is possible that its prevalence amongst the more highly evolved organisms should be considered in part as a result of an inherently determined evolution of the natural selective system, but this is perhaps doubtful.

A great deal more can be said about the evolution of the genetic system. Darlington has discussed this at considerable length. The most primitive genetic system one can imagine would consist simply of a particle which possessed two capacities: firstly, that of reproducing itself or causing its reproduction; and secondly, that of mutating into new forms which were also capable of reproducing themselves in their new condition. It is possible that, in some of the simplest viruses and virus-like particles known in plants, we may have representatives of this very elementary situation. However, in most of the simplest organisms, such as the majority of viruses and bacteria, we already find a somewhat more complex system, in which several such particles appear to be joined together to form a linear chain. According to present knowledge, such chains normally consist of nucleic acid combined with protein, but it is thought that it is the former compound which carries the essential specificity which is transmitted during the self-reproduction of the material. Nucleic acid is built up from sequences of nucleotide groupings, each of which is composed of a purine or pyramidine base, united with a sugar and a phosphate group. It appears that in general two linear sequences of these groupings are coiled round one another in a double helix to form an extended nucleic acid chain.

The process of mutation, which is essential before any evolution can take place, appears to involve an alteration in the purine or pyramidine bases at one or more link in the chain. Evidence is gradually accumulating that, in the most elementary case, only a single link is involved. This evidence, which in any case is not yet conclusive, is being gathered in the main from studies on the simplest types of organisms such as viruses. It is conceivable that the mutations which we normally consider when dealing with the evolution of the higher forms may involve a more complex process, and that there has been an evolution of the nature of mutation. We should have to suppose that this was so if we came to the conclusion that the chromosomes of higher animals and plants are more complex in their structure than the simple nucleic acid double helices which we encounter in viruses and bacteria. As yet, there seems to be no compelling reason for such a conclusion.

Even if the mutational process has not evolved from the condition in which it is in the viruses, the genetic system as a whole has certainly done so in the majority of higher forms. In all animals and plants, including protozoa, the hereditary endowment of a species includes a very large number of different and separable hereditary determinants or genes. At a very early stage in the evolution of living things, the genetic system evolved to a condition which on the one hand makes it possible to ensure that all offspring will be provided with all the necessary genes, and on the other allows for the shuffling and recombination of genes which may be present within a population.

This result was achieved by the well-known mechanism based on the presence of a diploid number of chromosomes in the cells of the body of the adult, their reduction to the haploid number in the formation of gametes, and sexual reproduction involving two parents. Darlington and others have discussed in detail the great evolutionary efficiency of this grade of organization of the genetic system. Indeed it is so efficient that, after it had occurred, no further anagenesis of an opening type has happened in relation to the hereditary distribution of nucleo-protein materials from one generation to the next. We are confronted in fact with one of the most striking examples of stasigenesis in the living world. There have, of course, been many evolutionary modifications of the genetic system in particular groups of animals and plants, for instance, by the development of a unisexual (parthenogenetic) or hermaphrodite reproduction, the partial or complete suppression of the crossing-over mechanism of gene recombination, and so on. But all such changes have been of a closing type, leading to restrictive specializations rather than opening new possibilities of advance.

The only opening anagenesis in the mechanism of the transference of information from one generation to the next which has occurred subsequent to the evolution of the diploid sexual reproductive system has not dealt with the distribution of nucleoprotein determinants, but has affected other mechanisms of information transfer, which may be referred to as paragenetic. This has led to the evolution of the characteristically human socio-genetic system of transmission and has been discussed above.

As to the epigenetic system, our understanding of it is still too fragmentary to support a full discussion of its evolution. We understand something of the general nature of the fundamental basic mechanism involved. This must be a circular interaction between genes and cytoplasm, by which the former determine the specificity of protein molecules being synthesized in the cell, while the cytoplasm is immediately responsible for deciding which complexes of genes shall be active.[1]

In the more highly evolved organisms, the development of such part-systems as muscles, nerve cells, glandular cells and so on, involves the simultaneous and co-ordinated operation of very large numbers of genes. On the other hand, in very lowly organisms, such as bacteria, most of the developmental situations which have been studied from a genetical point of view have involved the formation of single substances, such as enzymes, and in these cases only a small number of genes is usually in operation, and these seem to act with considerable independence of one another. At first sight one gets the impression that evolution has involved the appearance of more complex and more highly organized systems of genes. If one compares, for instance, a mammal with a bacterium, this conclusion is probably justified enough. But, in the first place, the anagenesis of the gene complexes may well be merely a secondary result of the increase in complexity of the adult organism, rather than any independent evolution of the epigenetic system on its own; and

[1] Waddington, 1954.

secondly, in organisms only slightly higher up the evolutionary scale than bacteria, we already meet complex components, such as the muscle-fibre systems or the gullet of protozoa. We cannot yet be at all confident in asserting that the genetic determination of such components in protozoa is any less complex than that of similar part-systems in higher organisms. Thus there is not very much evidence for any noteworthy evolution of the most basic epigenetic mechanisms.

The interaction between genes and the local cytoplasm is in many, perhaps in all, of the higher organisms complicated by the influence of diffusing substances passing from one region of the developing embryo to another. The most striking examples are the evocator substances in vertebrates, which are responsible for the phenomenon known as embryonic induction. Moreover, it seems very likely, though it is perhaps not finally demonstrated, that in all cases in which we see a single unified organ being formed out of a mass of tissue—in all cases in which we have what I have called an 'individuation field'—the orderly pattern in which the parts of the organ are arranged in relation to one another is the result of the diffusion of substances through the mass. Mechanisms of this kind, which depend on the movement of active substances from one part of the developing tissue to another, are only slightly less basic than the gene-cytoplasm interactions which were discussed above. Here again we have no conclusive evidence for an evolution of these types of mechanisms between the lowest and the highest organisms in the evolutionary scale. The development of the vertebrates certainly provides many examples of processes in which inductive and field relations are important, but so does that of such a lowly group as the Coelenterates.

It is, perhaps, not to be expected that these very fundamental epigenetic mechanisms would exhibit great evolutionary changes. They operate during the very earliest phases of the development of the embryo, and this is before natural selection makes itself most strongly felt. It is the later processes of development, in which an animal reacts to and perhaps becomes modified by its environment, that are likely to be more closely involved in evolution. For instance, mice reared in high temperatures tend to grow long tails, which may assist them in dissipating surplus body heat; tadpoles reared in water poor in oxygen develop larger gills, and many other similar examples could be given. One would expect from first principles that there has been a gradual evolution of more and more efficient mechanisms for carrying out modifications of this kind, and for ensuring that those modifications which are produced are of a kind which is useful to their possessor. However, so far as I know, sufficient facts are not yet available to validate this *a priori* deduction. We are still almost totally ignorant of the mechanisms by which adaptive epigenetic modifications come into being. It is a field which would repay much more study.

It is when we turn to consider the evolution of the exploitive system that we find ourselves confronting for the first time the whole mass of data which constitutes the major part of our knowledge of the course of evolution. The great corpus of information which forms the sciences of comparative anatomy, comparative physiology, comparative behaviour and ecology is almost entirely a description of the results of the evolution of the exploitive system, and when people use the phrase 'the results of evolution' it is usually the evolution of this system which they have in mind.

It was in relation to this material that the notions of anagenesis, stasigenesis and cladogenesis were first introduced. It is clear that for a discussion of biological evolution in relation to man and human evolution, it is the occurrence of anagenesis which takes the centre of the stage. Stasigenesis is in some ways a failure of evolution. When it occurs, the evolutionary processes have not succeeded in bringing about modification, which is their normal result; and if nothing but stasigenesis had happened in the organic world, the concept of evolution would never have been invented. Cladogenesis—the appearance of diversity—is, of course, a real evolutionary phenomenon. The notion could indeed be taken to cover the whole of evolution, if we were convinced that no anagenesis had occurred. If there are any biologists who, while accepting the notion of evolution, reject that of evolutionary progress, they must presumably consider that all the results of evolution can be placed under this heading. Such a position would, however, be a very extreme and peculiar one, so far removed from a simple interpretation of the evidence that one could scarcely avoid the suspicion that anyone advancing it was doing so merely in order to provide grounds for some future argument. I think that all biologists who have no ulterior ends in view have always, from the time of Aristotle, agreed that one can discern a real hierarchy or progression in the forms of the organic world.

Moreover, there is general agreement on at least the broad outlines of the way the hierarchy is arranged. At the bottom we have such elementary organisms as bacteria and viruses; immediately above them protozoa; then, to consider animals only, groups such as the sponges and coelenterates. Above them are a number of invertebrate groups—molluscs, echinoderms, a variety of types of worms, etc. There is plenty of room for debate as to the hierarchical arrangement of these groups, but each group contains within itself a variety of types which can usually be placed rather clearly in a hierarchical order. For instance, the cephalopods are a more advanced type of mollusca than the gasteropods. Again, it was probably one of the groups of worms which gave rise to the arthropods, which are unanimously recognized as being a higher group; and amongst the arthropods themselves, the insects, for instance, are certainly in some real sense hierarchically above, for instance, the crustacea. Finally, the group of vertebrates is certainly more advanced than any of the invertebrate groups; and within the vertebrates we can recognize a clear progression from various types of fish through the amphibia to the reptiles, birds and mammals.

The existence of a clear-cut hierarchical order, which we interpret as evolutionary anagenesis, within single groups such as the arthropods, forces us to remind ourselves of the distinction between opening and closing anagenesis. Evolution from a primitive anthropod to a highly evolved insect such as a fly or bee has undoubtedly involved the real improvement of the arthropod type of organization, but this improvement has at the same time brought with it limitations which render indefinite further improvements impossible. For instance, insects have adopted and brought to a high degree of perfection the system of aerating their tissues by means of small tubes leading in from the exterior, through which oxygen passes by the process of diffusion. This system can be extremely satisfactory when the distance which the oxygen has to travel is small; but it would be almost impossible to evolve from it a respiratory system which would serve the needs of animals much bulkier than the largest insects already are. Now, this limitation of the total volume of the body clearly limits the size, and therefore the possible complexity, of the nervous system. One cannot see any way in which an insect could evolve a brain as large as that of a human being. Although there is probably no precise relation between the size of the brain and the complexity of mental processes, they undoubtedly go roughly in parallel with one another. It seems almost certain that in adopting and perfecting their particular mode of supplying their tissues with oxygen, the insects have cut themselves off from the possibility of evolving a highly complex nervous apparatus.

Similar considerations probably apply to all the major groups of the animal kingdom. In each of them evolution has produced, by anagenesis, the improvement of one particular type of biological organization, but in doing so has gradually eliminated various other possibilities. Within each group anagenesis has been in the main closing anagenesis.

Evolutionary transitions from one major type of biological organization to another seem in general to have taken place at a very early stage in life's history on this earth, at a time when anagenesis within the groups had not proceeded very far. For the invertebrate groups, evidence concerning these changes is scanty. We know most about them in connection with the evolution which has taken place within the vertebrates. There the evidence suggests that the types of fish which gave rise to amphibia, the types of amphibia from which the reptiles arose, and the reptiles which evolved into mammals, were in every case relatively unspecialized representatives of their class. Anagenesis which leaves open the possibility of future advance cannot, it seems, proceed very far in the perfection of one particular type of organization.

The major point about opening anagenesis, which is important to the thesis I am advancing here, is that it has occurred. This I take to be established by the consensus of general biological opinion. It is another matter, although of course an important one, to try to formulate a general description of the overall direction in which the anagenetic change has been manifest. Many attempts have been made to do this; none of them is wholly satisfactory. The evolution of living things confronts us with a vast and complex array of results. It must always be to some extent a matter of choice and of judgment to attempt to isolate certain dominant trends from among the many different types of order which are implicit in the material. Some points of view have undoubtedly been too simple; for instance, Herbert Spencer suggested that the dominant anagenetic trend was a mere increase in complexity, but it is clear that this is very often a feature of closing rather than opening anagenesis.

Some of the best recent discussions have been given by Julian Huxley.[1] He lays particular stress on two factors of the animal's relation to its environment: firstly, the attainment of increasing independence of the environment, for instance, by the evolution of systems of maintaining a constant body temperature and so on; and secondly, the ability to control the environment. With the formulation of the latter point I am not in complete agreement. There are, after all, few organisms other than man that can do very much to control their environment. I should prefer to say that there is an increasing ability to utilize for the maintenance of life more and more complex relations between environmental variables.[2] Another way of phrasing this would be to say that if you try to account for the behaviour of an animal throughout its life in terms of the items of the environment to which it reacts, in the more highly evolved forms the number of these items would be greater than in a less evolved form, and the functional relation between the items to which the behaviour was related would also be more complex. One instance in which this principle is brought to expression is of course the evolution of more complex sense organs. Another is the increasing elaboration of the nervous system, and in particular the evolution of a

[1] Cf. for instance, 1942.
[2] Cf. Waddington, 1946.

centralized and increasingly complex brain.

The capacity to remain relatively independent of the environment, to incorporate into the life-system more complex functions of environmental variables, and ultimately to control the environment, all of course reach a much higher point in man than in any pre-human species. Even if we formulate the open anagenesis of the animal world in some way other than that adopted here, it would be impossible to conceal the fact that the evolution of the human race has carried forward in many respects sequences of change which we can see running through the sub-human world. During the history of the human race these changes have been brought about, in the main, by the influence of the characteristically human socio-genetic system. In the next chapter we must turn to consider in more detail the nature of this system, and in particular we must return to our main theme of ethics, by investigating the place which ethical beliefs have in the structure of human evolutionary mechanism.

CHAPTER 12

The Evolution of the Socio-genetic System

AS we have seen, the human species differs from the rest of the animal world in the fact that the greater part of its evolution is brought about by a system which depends on a socio-genetic mechanism for transmitting information from one generation to the next. It is now time to consider in more detail how this socio-genetic system operates, and the way in which ethical beliefs are implicated in it.

Any system for passing information from one entity to another must involve at least two elements, which may be referred to as a transmitter and a receiver, as well of course as a third element which constitutes the message. When hereditary qualities are handed on from one generation to the next by the biological mechanism, the message is carried by the gametes, the parents constitute the transmitters, and the offspring the receivers. We know a great deal—it is described in any good text-book of biology—about the processes involved in this transmission, such as the preparation of the gametes and their liberation from the bodies of the parents; and also about the processes of reception, namely, the coming together of the two gametes in fertilization, the union of the nuclei to constitute the zygote, etc. In the case of socio-genetic transmission of information our knowledge is much less complete. Nevertheless it is not too difficult to find extended discussions of some of the processes involved in the transmission end of the system. Philosophers have for long concerned themselves with the formation of concepts and their expression in language, that is to say their conversion into a potentially transmissible form. Less attention is usually paid to the processes by which such messages may be received, but this is, from the present point of view, the more important end of the picture.

The recipient of a socially transmitted message is commonly said to learn what the message conveys. The concept of learning is, however, a very wide one, which includes several rather different types of process. In the sub-human animal world, learning of some form or other is a comparatively common occurrence. There has been, and still is, a great deal of discussion as to how the various types of learning should be classified and related to one another.[1] For the purposes of a very general survey, which is all that is necessary here, one can be content to consider the three categories of conditioned reflex learning, exploratory learning and social learning. The first type depends on a repetition of some situation in which the animal is offered a choice of alternative ways of behaving, one of these types of behaviour having as a consequence something which can be broadly regarded as a reward, or alternatively as a punishment. It is frequently found that after a number of repetitions of the situation, the animal begins to behave consistently in the rewarding manner. The setting-up of conditioned reflexes can occur even in very simple, lowly-organized animals. It is, indeed, doubtful whether there has been much evolutionary improvement in the capacity for forming conditioned reflexes during the evolutionary advance from simple invertebrate types to the more advanced vertebrates, although of course the types of situation to which the animals can become conditioned does become more complex as their sensory and nervous equipment becomes able to deal with more complicated stimuli. The very simplest animals such as flatworms can learn to make a choice between right and left or between various pairs of elementary stimuli such as different temperatures or light intensities, while highly evolved animals such as the elephant can learn to discriminate between quite complex patterns.[2] In this context, it is not the process of learning itself which has advanced during evolution but only the nature of what is learnt.

I use the phrase 'exploratory learning' to cover cases in which the animal's behaviour is rather too complex to be easily accommodated within the category of conditioned reflex learning. The

[1] For instance, see Thorpe, Harlow and Hilgard.
[2] Rensch, 1957.

139

expression 'gestalt' learning has sometimes been used for certain
of these cases, but carries an implication of a particular psychological theory; 'latent learning' and 'insight learning' are other
names which have been employed. A classical example is perhaps
that of Kohler's ape Sultan, who discovered how to fit two
bamboo sticks together to make a longer tool by which he could
reach a banana which was originally just out of his reach. Other
examples are the birds which in Britain and northern Europe
learned for themselves to remove the metal caps from milk
bottles so as to get at the contents, or again the chimpanzees in
a California zoo who were observed to have discovered how to
operate a mechanical drinking fountain.[1]

It is difficult to draw any sharp line between the simpler forms
of exploratory learning and conditioned reflex learning. But such
evidence as we have suggests that the capacity for exhibiting
more highly developed types of exploratory learning increases as
we go up the evolutionary scale. It is only in such highly evolved
creatures as birds and mammals, and particularly primates, that
we meet really striking examples of it. Our knowledge of behaviour in the invertebrates is still so scanty that one would not
like to be certain that complex examples of exploratory learning
will not be discovered in them also but at present this seems
rather unlikely.

By social learning, I refer to cases in which one animal learns
from another or from man. In some cases, the learning may be
based on a straightforward imitation by the student of the
performances of his teacher. An example would be the learning
by parrots and other birds to imitate the sounds made by human
speakers. This might be described as 'exhibitive learning'. A
rather different process—'instructional learning'—is one in
which an animal learns to respond to certain actions or gestures
which it accepts as commands. Rensch, for instance, showed that
trained elephants may respond to a score or so of different words
of command from their mahout, and sheepdogs also accept an
extensive 'vocabulary' of words, whistles and gestures.

Bateson, writing from an anthropological point of view, and
after him several students of animal behaviour (e.g. Harlow),

[1] Hebb and Thompson, 1954.

have drawn attention to the importance of processes by which an individual, through the learning of one lesson, becomes better at learning the next. For such 'learning-to-learn' Bateson uses the expression 'deutero-learning', while Harlow speaks of 'set learning'. It is certain that effects of this kind can be detected in the higher mammals, and they are well developed in primates, but rather little is known about them in lower animals. The capacity for deutero-learning has almost certainly considerably increased during the course of evolution. It seems rather likely, indeed, that deutero-learning, at least in its advanced forms, involves the activity of the cerebral cortex, an organ whose increase in size during evolution is one of the most outstanding features of comparative anatomy.[1]

Whenever social learning comes into play between animals of the same species, the possibility is created of the transmission of information from one generation to the next. This has certainly occurred in some sub-human animals; for instance, the habit of opening milk bottles and drinking the contents is spreading within the bird population of Britain, and it seems certain that the mechanism of spread is by means of social learning rather than by the independent discovery of the principles of opening milk bottles by a series of individual exploratory acts of learning. Similarly, other chimpanzees learnt the trick of operating the drinking fountain in the California zoo from those individuals who had discovered it first. We have therefore in the infra-human world the possibility of the appearance of an elementary form of a socio-genetic mechanism of information transfer between the generations. It is important to consider both the similarities and the differences between these animal socio-genetic systems and the much more highly elaborated human one.

It is clear that any type of socio-genetic system involves as its most essential feature a process of communication between individuals. Animals may communicate with one another in a number of different ways, for instance, by bodily actions or by sounds. These actions or sounds may sometimes function simply

[1] For a good non-technical discussion of the functions of the central nervous system in learning, see J. Z. Young, *Doubt and Certainty in Science*.

as models to be imitated. This is presumably the case in the transmission of the habit of opening bottle caps. Again, Thorpe has shown that although there is usually a strong genetic determination of the sequence of notes and overall pattern in a bird's song, the strength of this determination varies from species to species and in some cases a young fledgling reared in the presence of birds of a different species, will, to a greater or lesser extent, learn the song of its foster parents. Here again, the transmitted element—the song of the parent—seems to be functioning simply as something to be imitated. In other examples of animal communication the transmitted element functions not as a model to be mimicked, but as a command or exhortation. Many species of animals emit cries or carry out actions which serve as signals of warning or of readiness to mate, etc. A great deal of interest has been aroused recently by the discovery of an extremely elaborate signal system of this kind amongst such comparatively lowly evolved creatures as the bees. Von Frisch has described how bees returning from a newly-discovered source of food will, on their return to the nest, perform a 'dance'; this involves running in a certain pattern with associated movements of the abdomen and wings, and the whole complex movement instructs their fellows to seek food at a certain distance from the hive in a specified direction.

Students of animal behaviour seem to be agreed that there is a radical difference between all such examples of animal communication and the language system of communication which is characteristic of the human species.[1] The distinction is usually expressed in terms of the concepts of signs and symbols, all animal communication involving only the former whereas man makes use of symbols as well as signs. A very good discussion of the meanings to be attached to these two words is that given by Langer. A sign is a transmitted element (word, noise, gesture, etc.) which can serve to evoke an appropriate action. In human life, for instance, the ringing of one kind of bell may be the sign that somebody is at the front door, of another kind of bell that somebody is on the telephone, of a third kind that a funeral is in progress and so on. 'In an ordinary sign function,' she says, 'there

[1] See, for instance, Mowrer and Thompson.

142

are three essential terms: subject, sign and object. In denotation, which is the simplest kind of symbol function, there have to be four: subject, symbol, conception and object.' A symbol, in fact, relates not simply to an object or action but essentially refers to a conception, that is to say, to an idea which can be thought about for its own sake. An important element in the functioning of a symbol is to give the name of such an idea. Langer writes: 'True language begins only when a sound keeps its reference beyond the situation of its instinctive utterance, e.g. when an individual can say not only: "My love, my love!" but also: "He loves me— he loves me not." Even though Professor Yerkes' young apes, Chim and Panzee, met their food with exclamations like "Kha!" or "Nga!" they are like a cry of "Yum, yum!" rather than: "Banana today." They are sounds of enthusiastic assent, of a very specialized emotional reaction; *they cannot be used between meals to talk over the merits of the feast.*'

Even the elaborate sign communication system of the bees should not be regarded as a true language since there is no evidence that the elements in it act as names of conceptions which exist independently of the actual situation. The bees, so far as we know, cannot discuss, sitting in the hive, the geographical information which the dances convey. Similarly, there is nothing to suggest that elephants or sheepdogs which have learnt to respond to a vocabulary of human words can accept these words as names of conceptions which can be arranged in new patterns. The words are functioning for them as signs, not, so far as we know, as symbols. The sort of evidence one would look for to detect the earliest stages in the development of symbolic functioning would be perhaps something as follows. Suppose an elephant had been taught a sign consisting of two words A and B, which together meant 'Lie down on your left side' and another sign of two other words C and D which meant 'Blow water on your right side'. Then, if when it first heard the combination A and D it responded by lying down on its right side, one might say that A and D had begun to function as symbols for the conceptions of lying down and right side respectively.

As a matter of fact, Rensch's elephants did show some traces of behaviour of this kind, not (as far as he has described the situation) in respect of sound, but in connection with the discrimination of patterns learnt as conditioned reflexes. He trained an elephant to select a card marked with a large, symmetrical black cross. When it was then tested with a number of other patterns, the animal was rather successful in choosing, out of a number of alternative patterns offered to him, those which contained crosses, even when these were of a different size to that on which he had originally been trained and were quite asymmetrical in shape. One may say that he had to some extent acquired the conception of a black cross. He was not able, however, to associate this with a white cross on a black background. Again, a trained elephant can distinguish cards containing three from those with four dots, even when the dots are arranged sometimes in one pattern, sometimes in another.[1]

We have, then, evidence for at least a beginning of the development of conceptions in the mental functioning of sub-human animals. In the present state of our scanty knowledge, the evidence for the existence of conceptions is strongest in cases in which there is little evidence of accompanying communication. We find traces of one element in symbol functioning without the other necessary accompanying factors.

Pumphrey has distinguished three characteristics in which human verbal symbols differ from the signs of animal communication. These are, firstly, detachment which allows men to discuss events without necessarily taking any action in connection with them; secondly, extensibility in time which makes possible reference to times past and future as well as times present; and thirdly, economy by which one symbol can stand for something which would otherwise require a long·elaborate description.

It may be that in the next few years observation of more highly evolved animals, and particularly of primates, will reveal situations in which we can discern a simultaneous functioning at an elementary level of all the factors involved in human symbolic communication. It seems certain, however, that although the gap between the human and the sub-human may be further narrowed, there will remain an enormous interval amounting to a qualita-

[1] Birds can also react to the abstract quality of number. Cf. O. Köhler, 1950.

tive change between man and his nearest sub-human relatives.

The magnitude of this gap probably depends largely on the fact that all human races, even those living under extremely primitive conditions, have more or less completely developed language systems. 'The outstanding fact about any language,' according to Edward Sapir, 'is its formal completeness. This is as true of any primitive language, like Eskimo or Hottentot, as of the carefully recorded and standardized languages of our great cultures. . . . It would be absurd to say that Kant's "Critique of Pure Reason" could be rendered forthwith into the unfamiliar accents of Eskimo or Hottentot, and yet it would be absurd in but a secondary degree. What is really meant is that the culture of these primitive folk has not advanced to the point where it is of interest to them to form abstract conceptions of a philosophical order. But it is not absurd to say that there is nothing in the formal peculiarities of Hottentot or Eskimo which would obscure the clarity or hide the depth of Kant's thought—indeed it may be suspected that the highly synthetic and periodic structure of Eskimo would more easily bear the weight of Kant's terminology than his native German.' Similarly, Whorf has suggested that the language of the Hopi Indians of south-western United States, which does not involve the notion of dimensional time, might be more appropriate than European languages for dealing with Einsteinian physics.

This remarkable efficiency of even primitive languages, which seem to lack nothing but vocabulary, has occasioned some surprise. For instance, Macdonald Critchley writes: 'Even in the case of the most untutored, primitive and savage human communities, the language system is so far removed in its comlexity from the crude and simple utterances of the sagest of the primates, as to be scarcely comparable. And nowhere and at no time has there been any hint of an approximation between these two extremes. . . . Can it be, therefore, that a veritable rubicon does exist between animals and man after all? . . . Can it be that Darwin was in error when he regarded the differences between man and animals as differences merely in degree?'

Langer also found very surprising the absence of undeveloped language systems among the races of man. It would appear to the biologist, however, that the situation is quite comparable to that of the gaps between the major phyla or families in the animal kingdom. Essentially the situation seems to be that certain new patterns of organization carry with them such great natural selective advantages that once they have developed to a certain pitch of effectiveness their competitive efficiency rapidly leads to the disappearance of the stages which led up to them. The development of a language system brings into being a new socio-genetic mechanism of evolution. It seems probable that the efficiency of this system would increase rapidly as the language system began to be formed and would gradually reach a period of diminishing returns after the language had reached a pitch of considerable perfection. If this were the case, highly developed language systems would rapidly drive out of existence the remaining examples of undeveloped ones. Thus, at the present time, after language has been in existence for a period which is long in terms of the working of man's socio-genetic evolutionary system, we should not expect to find that any of the early stages in the formation of language had still been able to persist.

For the content which in man is passed from one individual to another by the use of language symbols it is conventional and convenient to use the word 'culture'. This word has passed through many vicissitudes, even in the recent past. Sometimes it is employed in a restricted sense, to apply only to what we regard as the higher flights of civilization but this usage is becoming less common at least in scientific circles.[1] Archaeologists use it with particular emphasis on the material possessions—the 'material culture'—of a people. But it should be noted that the material artefacts of a human society are by no means independent of the content of their verbal interchanges. This is well brought out by considering the definition of man which is generally accepted by palaentologists and students of stone implements. Man, they say, can be described as the primate which

[1] See, for instance, T. S. Eliot, *Notes Towards the Definition of Culture*, Faber & Faber, London, 1948. Eliot uses the word in a sense in which he can write: 'The "conditions of culture" which I set forth do not necessarily produce the higher civilization: I assert only that when they are absent, the higher civilization is unlikely to be found.'

makes tools of definite and standardized patterns.[1] Every part of this definition is necessary. The criterion must be tool-making, not tool-using, since many lower animals (for instance, one of the species of Darwin's Galapagos finches or the Californian sea-otter[2]) may use natural objects as tools. Again, some non-primates make artefacts which can be regarded as tools and which are of standardized patterns, for instance, birds' nests. Finally, some primates, such as apes, may make tools but to non-standardized patterns, such as by fitting sticks together or breaking a stick to a convenient length. But man makes tools to a standardized pattern; and the standardization is not laid down by inherited instinct, as in birds, but is transmitted to him through the mechanisms of social communication. Thus, his material culture is a manifestation of the content of the communications being carried on in his society.[3]

We may then say that with the achievement of speech employing verbal symbols man reached a stage at which he developed a culture. In his societies the socio-genetic mechanism of transmission of information from one generation to the next operates at a cultural level. It is a cultural socio-genetic mechanism. In the simpler social systems of sub-human animals, there may, as we have seen, be some rudimentary form of socio-genetic transmission but this involves only mechanisms of a simpler nature than culture. Hallowell speaks of them as proto-cultural.

What are the requirements in individual mental functioning which are necessary before a man or animal can function as a unit in a system of cultural or proto-cultural socio-genetic transmission? And how, if at all, are these necessary characteristics related to the development of ethical systems?

Probably a considerable number of prerequisites could be enumerated. My purpose here is not to evaluate all the suggestions that have been made[4] but rather to present the case for

---

[1] Quoting L. S. B. Leakey.

[2] E. Fisher, 1939.

[3] Cf. Dennis Oakley, 1951, where a distinction is made between the improvization of tools and their systematic manufacture.

[4] In particular, I shall make no attempt to review the extensive literature on social behaviour in animals; some recent reviews are the articles by Thompson, 1958; Emerson, 1958; Scott, 1956; and Tinbergen, 1953.

regarding one particular psychological modification—what I shall describe as the formation of authority-bearing systems within the mind—as among the essential steps that have to be taken during evolution before cultural socio-genetic transmission becomes possible. But in order to provide some background against which this suggestion can be more clearly seen it may be useful to consider the points made by Hallowell in a recent very valuable review, in which he has considered much of the literature concerning socialization and made suggestions concerning the relation between this process and the development of value systems.

Hallowell sees the first requisite for social behaviour in a function which he describes as 'role differentiation'. 'The infra-hominid type of social structure is linked to the biological fact that a basic function is involved—the procreation and nurture of offspring helpless, not only at birth but for considerable periods afterwards. The structure of the group is determined by the roles which the adult members of both sexes play towards each other and their offspring.' Hallowell is here speaking of the infra-hominid apes. In still lower groups of the animal kingdom there are, of course, many social systems which are not linked to the procreation and nurture of offspring, for instance, wolf packs, shoals of fish, flocks of starlings, or herds of deer outside the breeding season. But in all these, as well as in other reproductive societies such as the nesting colonies of sea birds so fully studied by Tinbergen and others, or the more dispersed arrangement of breeding individuals found, for instance, in the robins studied by Lack, it remains true that the functioning of the society depends on an individual behaving, when he meets another, in a manner appropriate to some role or other. For instance, when one robin intrudes into the territory of another, one of the pair behaves as an owner and the other as a trespasser. In a herd of feeding deer,[1] one will act as the sentinel and the others as the guarded who expect his warning. The social organization implies, as Hallowell states, the existence of more or less alternative roles, one or other of which an individual will assume at a particular moment, and in a particular context.

[1] Fraser Darling, 1937.

Hallowell then goes on to consider some of the implications of role differentiation and their relation to the appearance of systems which involve ethical values: 'If the essence of any kind of social order rests upon role differentiation, the essence of a moral order is characterized by the fact that role differentiation is mediated through socialized values and goals acquired by organisms capable both of self-awareness and of making choices between courses of action with reference to socially sanctioned goals and values. The principle common to both levels of social organization is that role behaviour on the part of individuals is, within limits, predictable in a wide variety of situations. This is what makes it possible to establish empirically characteristic patterns of behaviour interaction, whether in invertebrates, vertebrates or primates, despite the fact that the relative importance of innate versus learned determinants may vary widely at different levels. Thus, moral orders in *homo sapiens* are functionally equivalent to the non-moral orders in lower primates, as well as in other animals, in so far as they may be considered an effective means in promoting and maintaining systems of social action.'

In this passage Hallowell expresses a part of the point that I am attempting to establish. He suggests that moral orders in *homo sapiens* are an essential functional part of his type of social organization. Exactly how they are essential and exactly what part they play is, however, left rather vague. Hallowell proceeds only to describe a further necessary condition which must be fulfilled before a moral order can exist. 'The functioning of a social system as a moral order requires a capacity for self-objectification on the part of the actor, self-identification with his own conduct over time, and appraisal of his own conduct and that of others in a common framework of socially recognized and sanctioned standards of behaviour. Without a psychological level of organization that permits the exercise of these and other functions, moral responsibility for conduct could not exist, nor would any social structure function as a moral order.' Again, I agree that self-objectification, in the sense of recognizing a continuity of the self from one instant of time to another, is an essential requisite for the appearance of a moral system. Indeed,

I suspect it is essential, at least in some elementary form, even for role differentiation and possibly for learning, but a reference to it does not by any means exhaust what there is to say concerning the relations between moral systems and social behaviour.

The question I should like to ask is not, what are the prerequisites for a moral order; but rather what, over and above role discrimination and self-awareness, is necessary for the functioning of a socio-genetic system? And the factor to which I wish to draw attention is the necessity for the recognition, if you wish to express it so, of one particular role, namely, that of receiver or acceptor of socially-transmitted information. Societies may, of course, exist without the recognition of this role. We can have a social system organized around the roles of owner and trespasser, or guardian and guarded, or sexually active males and females, but if these were the only roles in the societies, no mechanism would be provided for the serial transmission of information down the generations, or at least this would only occur in a haphazard and chance manner and the content of the transmitted messages would be very low. Socio-genetic transmission requires not only role differentiation but specifically the recognition of the roles of the teacher and the taught. This appears to be a logical necessity. It is also an empirically observed fact, of great obviousness in the human cultural system and somewhat less obtrusive but still verifiable in sub-human societies.

The essential feature in the role of the taught, of the recipient of information, is to act as though under the authority of something. It may be that some other individual is acted towards as a model to be imitated, or as someone in command, whose signs are to be obeyed, or in the case of man, whose symbolic statements are to be accepted. In sub-human animal societies so far as we know the authority-bearing entity is always external to the recipient individual. This is no longer the case in man. We find, as an empirical fact, that man can as it were 'internalize' authority. He can with one part of his mental make-up play the role of the taught in relation to some other part which functions as the teacher. Conscience may, as we well know, become a stern internal authority. (There is considerable, though perhaps rather anecdotal, evidence that something of the same kind may happen in sub-human domestic animals which are in contact with man. Dogs, for instance, often show every sign of having a bad conscience, and my friend Margaret Mead assures me that the same is true of the intimately domesticated pigs of the Pacific Islands. If this is true, what man has acquired during evolution is not so much the faculty of being an acceptor of internalized authority, but rather that of being able to bring it about that his authority as a teacher becomes internalized by the taught.)

Be this as it may, the point I wish to stress is that the functioning of a socio-genetic system depends essentially on the existence of the role of authority-acceptor. In man the formation of this role is brought about by processes which involve the internalization of authority. And some aspects of this internalized authority have the character for which we give the name ethical. Thus 'going in for ethics', or 'ethicizing', is for man an integral part of the role of the taught or the authority-acceptor, without the existence of which his cultural socio-genetic evolutionary system could not operate.

It may perhaps appear at first sight that the authority necessary to ensure that a message is received can be derived from the world of fact, within which the content of the message can be verified—or, as another version would have it, within which the recipient fails to find anything which falsifies that content. It is unnecessary in the present connection to go into the difficulties of the concept of verification.[1] The point of immediate importance is that a great deal of social transmission takes place at a time when the recipient is much too young to apply any verification procedures, which must be regarded as relatively sophisticated mechanisms for adjustment and rectification rather than as

[1] It has been argued that it is logically impossible to verify a hypothetical statement, since if the statement is 'If P then Q' and we actually find Q, the initial statement did not exclude the alternative statement 'If R then Q'. Hence it is suggested that the important notion is that of falsification, since if we fail to find Q this falsifies the hypothesis. But it must be pointed out that the original statement also does not exclude 'If P and R, then not Q', which is *not* falsified. Logically, indeed, it seems probable that any hypothesis can be reconciled with any state of affairs by the invocation of suitable subsidiary hypotheses—a procedure for which it is not difficult to find examples in the history of science.

basic elements in the fundamental mechanism of transmission. Human social life is built up primarily on socially transmitted information which is accepted, rather than on information which has been tested and verified. If one compares social transmission with heredity, then verification is to be compared with natural selection. Just as the genic mechanism can transmit inefficient or even lethal genes, so the socio-genetic mechanism can transmit items of information which cannot be verified because they are factually untrue.

The processes by which the human authority system becomes formed and internalized will be discussed more fully in the next section. Here it is necessary to glance at the rather scanty information we have about similar processes in sub-human animals. In general our ignorance in this connection is extreme, but there are two types of phenomenon which are interesting and suggestive. The first is the well-known process of imprinting.[1] In several species of birds, such as ducks and geese, it is found that a young newly-hatched individual becomes profoundly attached to the first individual of its own species (or even of certain other species) it encounters. It is then said to be imprinted with this individual, whom it follows round and imitates and to whom it runs for refuge. Phenomena similar to imprinting have been seen in insects, fish and certain mammals as well as in birds. It does not, however, appear to be universal in social animals. For instance, it does not seem to be possible to cause imprinting in the domestic fowl, at least under laboratory conditions. Moreover, the ease with which it occurs varies in different races of ducks, and there is even some variation, which appears to be genetically controlled, within a single race. The mechanism by which the imprinting is brought about remains highly obscure. It occurs most easily during a short period soon after hatching. Auditory stimuli can be effective, though to a lesser degree than visual ones. Hess attributes particular importance to the degree of effort which must be exerted by the duckling during the imprinting period. In fact he goes so far as to formulate the relation that the strength of imprinting is proportional to the

[1] See, for instance, Lorenz, Thorpe and Hess. For general reviews of allied phenomena, see Beach, Jaynes and Hinde.

logarithm of the effort expended by the animal during this period.

We know, of course, nothing about the subjective experience of the imprinted duck. We can say only that it behaves as though the individual imprinted on it carries authority, or is worthy of 'respect', to use the word employed by Piaget in his work on the moral development in young children. It is interesting to note, however, that several investigators have described the attitude of the young animal to the older by which it is imprinted as an ambivalent one (cf. Hinde). The duckling reacts to its mentor not only with 'respect', as a source of reassurance, but also sometimes with fear, and eventually even with aggression. As we shall see in the next chapter, the relation of a human infant to its parent is also ambivalent; indeed, probably to an extreme degree, at least at an unconscious level. The parallelism is provocative, but men and birds are much too far removed from one another zoologically for it to be profitable to attempt any precise comparison between them in such a connection.

Another recent study which falls in the general area of the relations between authority-acceptors and authority-bearers in sub-human societies is the very interesting investigation by Harlow of the reaction of young Rhesus monkeys to various types of substitute mother. Having discovered that hand rearing of young monkeys in a zoo produced a better survival rate than natural feeding in these circumstances, Harlow proceeded to study what happened when suckling monkeys were provided with their food from bottles placed in crude mother models, made either out of welded wire mesh or of a similar material covered in soft Terry cloth. The interesting point emerged that the young monkeys behaved as though they greatly enjoyed, and obtained much reassurance from bodily contact with the soft cloth which covered one type of model; and they appeared to form a close emotional love attachment to it, whereas the bare wire model was treated merely as a source of nourishment and nothing else. The experiment has many implications, for instance, for child rearing practices. Its importance from our present point of view is that here we have another example of the formation in a sub-human animal of a relation of dependence between the receiving and what might be the transmitted ends of a socio-genetic transmission system. It can only be by the experimental investigation of situations such as this that we shall learn something about the nature of the authority-bearing and authority-accepting mental functions in the social systems of man's ancestors.

CHAPTER 13

Human Evolution and the Fall of Man

ANY discussion of how it comes about that the human personality can accept authority, and is thus enabled to function as a receiver for socially transmitted information must nowadays lean very heavily on the work of Piaget and of Freud and his successors.

Piaget studied the origin of the moral sense in young children both by observing their behaviour, and by cross-questioning them, but without attempting to penetrate into the deeper levels of their mental processes in the way psychoanalysts have done. The first point to note, in his conclusions, is that he decisively rejects the possibility that 'ethicizing' is the result of wholly innate properties which would be exhibited even by an individual who was brought up in isolation. 'For the real conflict,' he writes (p. 100), 'lies between those who want to explain the moral consciousness by means of purely individual processes (habit, biological adaptation, etc.) and those who admit the necessity for an inter-individual factor. Once grant that two individuals at least must be taken into account if a moral reality is to develop, then it matters not whether you describe the facts objectively, as Durkheim did, or at least tried to do, or whether you describe them in terms of consciousness.' And, as he points out a little later (p. 101): 'Before the intervention of adults or older children there are in the child's conduct certain rules which we have called motor rules. But they are not imperative, they do not constitute duties but only spontaneous regularities of behaviour.' This conclusion amounts to a rejection of the view that the fundamental ethical characteristic is a quality (a non-natural one, according to Moore) that we merely recognize, as we recognize, for instance, colour. Piaget's point is in agreement with the argument given above (p. 54) that in the genesis of the faculty of ethical belief an essential part is played by inter-

actions between the individual and factors in his external surroundings, particularly other persons.

Pursuing his enquiries into the stages of life-history in which
inter-personal relations become importance, Piaget points out
(p. 193) that 'There seem to exist in the child two separate
moralities, of which, incidentally, the consequences can also be
discerned in adult morality. These two moralities are due to
formative processes which, broadly speaking, follow on one
another without, however, constituting definite stages. . . . The
first of these processes is the moral constraint of the adult. . . .
The second is co-operation.' In both these processes, Piaget
argues that two conditions 'are necessary, and their conjunction
sufficient. 1. The individual must receive a command from
another individual; the obligatory rule is therefore psycholo-
gically different from the individual habit or from what we have
called the motor rule. 2. The individual receiving the command
must accept it, i.e. must respect the person from whom it came.'
In the first of the two processes, the individual who gives the
command and is respected is a parent, or other adult or older
child; in the second, it is a member of a group of equals to which
the recipient child has come to belong. To quote again Piaget's
own words (p. 102): 'It seems to us an undeniable fact that in
the course of the child's mental development, unilateral respect
or the respect felt by the small for the great plays an essential
part; it is what makes the child accept all the commands transmitted to him by his parents and is thus the great factor of continuity between different generations. But it seems to us no less
undeniable . . . that as the child grows in years the nature of his
respect changes. In so far as individuals decide questions on an
equal footing—no matter whether subjectively or objectively—
the pressure they exercise upon each other becomes collateral.
. . . It is necessary, in order to grasp the situation, to take
account of two groups of moral facts—constraint and unilateral
respect, on the one hand, co-operation and mutal respect on the
other.'

These quotations exhibit very clearly the great importance
which Piaget attaches to what he calls 'respect'. This name is, as
I shall hope to show by reference to the psychoanalytical results,

perhaps rather too pallid and innocent for the mental factor which is actually involved. Also, in emphasizing—as it is indeed necessary to do—the essential role of extra-individual environmental factors, Piaget has done less than justice to some of the internal innate characteristics of human beings which more recent authors have shown to be operative. But in the present connection the important point is the close similarity between the role which Piaget attributes to 'respect' and the role which has been assigned here to what I have called 'authority-bearing systems within the mind'. Piaget argues that such systems are essential for the first appearance of the moral consciousness; I am arguing that, in addition to fulfilling this function, they are also essential for disposing the newborn individual to be a recipient for socially transmitted 'information' in general—the word 'information' being used in the wide sense given to it in scientific theory.

It is during the first of Piaget's two periods that the child becomes an 'ethicizing' creature; and it is this period, therefore, rather than the second co-operative period, which is of particular interest in the context of this book. What is the nature of the 'respect' which appears at this stage, characterizing the relation between the child and its parents? Piaget realizes that 'respect', in its ordinary meaning at least, does not fully describe the situation he finds. 'It is a fact,' he writes (p. 379), 'that the child in the presence of his parents has the spontaneous feeling of something greater than and superior to himself. Thus respect has its roots deep down in certain inborn feelings and is due to a *sui generis* mixture of fear and affection which develops as a function of the child's relation to his adult environment.'

This is not a very specific description, but it is perhaps as good as can be expected to emerge from studies of the kind Piaget undertook. The feeling of 'respect' is a subjective phenomenon, and the only way to examine it narrowly is to use the methods of introspection or, better, the developed form of introspection which is commonly known as psychoanalysis. We must therefore now turn to consider some aspects of psychoanalytical theory.

Freud considered that the adult human personality comes into

being through a series of interactions between innate potentialities, internal to the individual, and various external circumstances, of which interpersonal contacts, particularly with parents
or parent-substitutes, are particularly important. The innate
potentialities become manifested in a sequence which arises in
the main from an inherent process of maturation. In the newborn infant, the only inborn characteristics which are functioning
are very general biological drives, such as those for food,
warmth, contact with 'comfortable' surfaces, etc.; Freud, pene-
trating behind the surface of obvious appearances, summarizes
them as strivings after self-preservation, love and (surprisingly
enough) self-destruction. At a rather later stage, other innate
characters emerge into operation. It is these which, in the well-
known Freudian theory, lead to the formation of the Oedipus
complex and penis envy.

Freud himself expounded the nature of these innate factors in
terms of biological theories which are nowadays outmoded. He
seems, in the first place, to have taken rather literally the old
cliche that an animal's ontogeny can be explained in terms of its
phylogeny. This is the 'theory of recapitulation', which we now
regard as at best a mode of description (and usually an in-
accurate one at that) which does not provide any sort of causal
explanation of individual development. Freud combined this
with a belief that acquired characters may be directly inherited,
in a truly Lamarckian manner. Using these two biological
theories, which were by no means unfashionable at the time he
was writing, Freud[1] suggested that the innate human character-

[1] This account of Freud's thought, which is based on that given by several of
his recent expositors, may actually do him something less than justice. Discussing
'The Return of Totemism in Childhood', in the last section of *Totem and Taboo*, he
writes: 'A part of the problem seems to be met by the inheritance of psychical
dispositions which, however, need to be given some sort of impetus in the life of
the individual before they can be roused into actual operation. This may be the
meaning of the poet's words (from Goethe's *Faust*):
  Was du ererbt von deinen Vätern hast,
  Erwirb es, um es zu besitzen.
('What thou hast inherited from thy fathers, acquire it to make it thine.')
What Freud is suggesting here—the mutual reinforcement in each generation of a
hereditary disposition and external circumstances—could be interpreted as not too
far removed from the ideas concerning the genetic assimilation of acquired
characters discussed in Chapter 9. However, it is true that he finishes his dis-

istics which give rise to the Oedipus complex were imprinted into mankind as a result of a real event which occurred among our phylogentic ancestors, in which the young men of a 'primitive horde' murdered their father in order to gain access to the women. Present day psychoanalytic theory takes a very different view. It traces the Oedipus complex to the peculiarities of man's highly unusual rate of development.[1] The human sexual organs reach a state at which they would appear capable of normal functioning by an age of about five or six, which is about the age of sexual maturity in apes and probably in man's ancestors; but in *homo sapiens* there then intervenes a period of 'latency' before overt sexual behaviour starts. No other animal exhibits this odd example of 'brinkmanship'—this coming to the edge of sexual maturity and then pausing for some years before crossing the threshold. It is to the psychological tensions set up during this phase of disharmony between what the body could do and does do that the Oedipus situation is nowadays attributed. Its explanation is thus still sought in the innate constitution of the human species, but the innate potentialities are no longer thought of as derived from phylogenetically acquired characters.

It has always been clear that the phases of personality-development in which the Oedipus situation is involved are not among the very earliest to occur; and the modern theories which argue that the Oedipus complex is intimately related to the period of latency makes it even more obvious that it arises too late to be directly relevant to the initial moulding of the new-born infant into an 'ethicizing' being. The original 'respect' or authority-hearing systems will be transfigured by the Oedipus situation before the adult stage is reached, but they must have come into being before latency occurs. It is their origin rather than their later transformations which is most relevant to the present argument.

In recent years the attention of psychoanalyses has been somewhat diverted from the problems of the initial phases of personal-

cussion with an emphasis on the importance of an initial historical event in the early history of the race: 'Im Anfang war die Tat', another quotation from Goethe. And in his later books, such as *The Future of an Illusion*, it is again the historical rather than the present fact on which he lays emphasis.

[1] Cf. for instance, G. Roheim, and M. Mead, 1960.

ity development. Freud and his immediate successors were deeply concerned with the nature of the mental factors which appear in the first year or two of life, most of which later become unconscious through processes of repression and the like. The last twenty years or so has been dominated by a new set of interests. Hallowell, who has given a useful summary of this trend of opinion, quotes Bellak as follows: 'The novelty in psychoanalysis was originally its introduction of the unconscious, in the sense of the unconscious of feelings, the unawareness of previously experienced events, the covert nature of motivations, and the hidden meaning of dreams and symptoms. Slowly the tension focused on the forces responsible for this unconsciousness, notably repression. . . . Now the pendulum has swung nearly full cycle, in that there is so much talk about ego psychology today that the forces of the unconscious are possibly already somewhat in disregard.' The whole of this movement, which is usually considered to have been initiated by Anna Freud's *The Ego and the Mechanisms of Defence* of 1936, finds its main interests in processes which happen long after the initiation of 'ethicizing'. Although, as was pointed out earlier (p. 27), one cannot make a clear-cut boundary between the period in which ethicizing originates and the period in which the authority-systems become elaborated, the bulk of the work of the modern movement in psychoanalysis has rather little bearing on the topic in which we are primarily interested.

The first stage in the development of the human personality is a state which has been described by Balint as 'a harmonious mix-up in our minds between ourselves and the world around us'. 'Through our clinical experiences,' he writes, ''we have arrived at a primitive picture of the world in which (a) there is complete harmony between the individual and environment; (b) the individual does not care and is not in a position to say where he ceases and the external world begins; and (c) neither can an external observer define exact boundaries. At this stage of development there are as yet no objects, although there is already an individual, who is surrounded, almost floats, in substances without exact boundaries; the substances and the individual mutually penetrate each other; that is, they live in a harmonious mix-up.' As Freud put it, 'Originally the ego in-cludes everything, later it detaches from itself the external world.'

Balint's essay, from which I have just quoted, was concerned with the process by which the notion of firmly bounded definite objects come into being, and in the sentences quoted he is con-trasting such objects with substances which have no precise boundaries or edges. He goes on to point out that 'the discovery that firm and separate independent objects exist destroys this world. From then on, in addition to substances, the existence of objects with their resistant, aggressive and ambivalent qualities must be accepted'. His discussion shows that even such a basic faculty of the human mind as the recognition of external objects is not an autonomous capacity with which the human being is from the beginning endowed. The realization that there exists a category of entities which can be called objects is produced by the interaction between the mind and things outside it, namely, its environment.

The same situation has been revealed by those who study the human mind by more direct methods than psychoanalysis. For instance, the anatomist J. Z. Young points out that 'to an un-expected extent our brain has to learn before we can even see things'. 'We have,' he writes, 'no means of examining and re-cording all that happens in the brains of babies and very young children. But we can learn a great deal that is helpful from the reports of people with certain rare forms of blindness who, though born blind, have later been operated on and received their sight. . . . He reports only a spinning mass of lights and colours. He proves to be quite unable to pick out objects by sight, to recognize what they are or to name them. . . . When shown a patch of one colour placed on another he will quickly see that there is a difference between the patch and its sur-roundings. What he will not do is to recognize that he has seen that particular shape before, nor will he be able to give it its proper name. . . . It takes at least a month to learn the names of even a few objects.'

If the brain has to be trained, by interaction with the environ-ment, to acquire the patterns of activity which correspond to the sense perception of separate defined external objects, how much more must this be the case for the formation of such complex things as authority-bearing systems? From its initial state of a solipsistic mix-up with the external world, the mind of a new-born infant progresses towards the fully developed condition in which psychoanalysts distinguish three component mental systems, the id, the ego and the superego. Throughout this developmental process, internal driving forces are operative, in the form of innate instincts. The gradual metamorphosis of these instincts into a mature personality is initiated by their conflict with the external world of what we may call, for these purposes, objective reality.

Some philosophers have claimed that man has an innate faculty for recognizing a quality which belongs in the ethical field, just as he has a faculty for recognizing colour. This is to employ a type of thinking which is outmoded in biology. We do not now consider it possible to make clear distinctions between activities or properties which are innate and those which are acquired. All characters of living things arise from the development of inborn potentialities in relation to the environmental circumstances. One cannot even say that for some characters the inborn factors are, in all contexts, more important than the external ones, while in other characters the situation is reversed. All that one can legitimately do is to compare the relative importance of internal and external factors in producing the variation in the character as one finds it in some definite assemblages of individuals. We may say, for instance, that if we compared the colour vision of a large number of more or less normal people we should expect to discover that any differences which appeared would be largely attributable to differences in innate potentialities. The conclusions of psychoanalysis are that in the genesis of 'ethicizing' activity in normal human beings, both the internal and the external factors are certainly important. But there is considerable controversy as to their relative contribution to the diversity in such activities which we encounter in the human species, and a biologist would, I think, suspect that many psychoanalysts and anthropologists in recent years have tended unduly to minimize the role of the innate factors. But the point which it is essential to emphasize in the present context is that the external factors have a very essential part to play.

This conclusion is of the greatest possible practical importance. If it were not so, and if we were endowed with a wholly inborn capacity to accept authority (including ethical authority), then the human socio-genetic mechanism of evolution would be as difficult to improve as the biological genetic system is. Man, like other animals, produces haploid gametes by the reduction division of certain cells of his body. Provided only that the conditions are such that healthy growth is possible, this mechanism will be developed and will operate; and it is, both in its general outline and its details, not in any way dependent on particular precipitating circumstances, but only on very general conditions of the environment. This means that even if we can think of some way to improve it—for instance, perhaps, by increasing the frequency of crossing-over—it would be exceedingly difficult to effect the change. The biological evolutionary machine must for all practical purposes be taken as given. The only freedom we have in respect to it is a degree of control over the frequency with which gametes are passed on to the next generation, and some choice—very imprecise it is true—as to the character of the gametes with which they will become united. Our situation with respect to the socio-genetic mechanism is much more favourable. The innate factors are not so nearly autonomous in determining the character of the authority-bearing systems which play such an essential role in this mechanism. They do no more than provide labile potentialities from which these systems may be developed; and the systems which in fact appear are essentially moulded by interactions between the individual and the environment which are potentially under human control. We can therefore, in fact we must, contemplate the improvement of the socio-genetic mechanisms; not merely the utilization of the mechanism to obtain other results, but an actual increase in the effectiveness with which the mechanism carries out its function.

Such an improvement of the mechanism is certainly very much to be desired. In the evolution of the particular manner in which moral authority is developed in the mind of man, God, as Freud said,[1] has been guilty of an 'uneven and careless piece of work'.

The intuition of mankind has always realized this. All the essential points are enshrined in the myth of Adam and Eve, whose plucking of the fruits of the Tree of Knowledge led to the Fall of Man. According to this story, man gains access to the socially-transmitted store of knowledge only at the cost of a process which involves also the consciousness of good and evil and the experience of the reproductive human family.[2] This cost is heavy. The authority which is necessary if man is to be a receiver of socially-transmitted messages seems to be produced by a mechanism which usually leads to its over-development. Without an internal system of authority an individual of the species *homo sapiens* could not become a human person, but the price he pays is to be inflicted, by the excessive development of authority, with feelings which are described as guilt, anxiety and despair. A mild expression of this dilemma is Balint's remark that 'being adult is tantamount to having ambivalent feelings'. A more extreme one, more in tune with the fashionable pessimism of our time, is Kierkegaard's statement from *Sickness Unto Death*: 'With every increase in the degree of consciousness, and in proportion to that increase, the intensity of despair increases: the more consciousness, the more intense the despair.'

Psychoanalysts have discussed extensively the mechanism by which systems having authority are formed within the mind, and the reasons why this process so often, though not inevitably, produces authority which is stronger and more demanding than would seem to be necessary. There is still, of course, considerable debate about the details of the process, but there seems to be general agreement on the one major and essential feature of it; that the authority tends to be personalized. It is formed by a process which involves something which can be very roughly described as letting into the mind an external personality, this external personality being derived partially from the persons with whom the child comes in contact, and partially by a com-

[1] Quoted from Kaplan.
[2] If the Fall of Man has any meaning within the field of evolutionary biology it must be in the context of reproduction rather than of copulation.

plex, two-way process of projection and re-introjection of the child's own personality.

The concept of personality is an extremely difficult one, and I do not propose to attempt to define exactly what we mean by the term. It seems rather likely that it is a name for a specific level of organization of mental processes, an emergent level which appears only at the human stage of evolution. We cannot, I think, conceive of a human person who does not include an authority-system, which enables him to act as a recipient of social information, and this system, as we have seen, is itself to some extent personalized. For our purposes, then, the concept of personality must be accepted as an irreducible, to the same extent (no more, as well as no less) as we accept the concept of a biological organism. A full exposition of what the term implies is the inevitably unattainable goal of our understanding of man, just as the full understanding of organism is the ultimate goal of biology. We find ourselves here again confronted with the task of unravelling a circular and not a merely sequential chain of causal relations; the development of the human infant into a person involves entities which are themselves, to some extent, persons.

The psychoanalytic theories of the processes by which a baby becomes a person are couched in terms of the three systems into which an adult mentality is analysed, namely the id, the ego and the super-ego. In the recent formulations, deriving from Anna Freud's work, the processes which go on when this development is fully under way can be envisaged as resulting from 'anxieties' of the ego. These are of three main kinds: objective anxiety, about situations in the external world; super-ego anxiety, about the demands of the super-ego; and instinctual anxiety, about the demands of the innate instincts, which by this time are mostly operating within the id. Against these anxieties, the ego adopts various methods of defence. There are many different kinds of defence mechanisms, any or all of which may be used against any of the anxieties. Many of these, however, can only be made use of after the developing individual has already become a rather well-differentiated person, in which id, ego and super-ego have reached a considerable degree of autonomous existence.

In the earliest phases of development during which the baby first becomes an ethicizing creature, the situation is simpler. In the first place, the super-ego is only in process of formation, and thus super-ego anxiety is not yet developed into a powerful force. Again, it appears to be the case that the instincts do not, at first, of themselves cause any mental tension of the kind that can be regarded as an anxiety. As Anna Freud writes (p. 61): 'The ego of a little child . . . does not combat the instincts of its own accord. . . . It regards the instincts as dangerous because those who bring the child up have forbidden their grtaification. . . . Its defence against them is motivated by dread of the outside world, i.e. by objective anxiety.' Thus, in this very early period, it is only one of the three types of anxiety which is of major importance. Moreover, only a few of the types of defence mechanism can be used against it. Repression and sublimation, for instance, cannot be carried out before the super-ego is adequately developed. Anna Freud suggests that the main weapons in the hands of the young baby are 'such processes as regression, reversal or turning round upon the self'. She also draws attention to the views of 'the English School', who suggest that 'introjection and projection, which in our (Anna Freud's) view should be assigned to the period after the ego has been differentiated from the outside world, are the very processes by which the structure of the ego is developed and but for which differentiation would never have taken place. These differences of opinion bring home to us the fact that the chronology of psychic processes is still one of the most obscure fields of analytical theory'.

In the years since Anna Freud wrote, understanding of these processes has undoubtedly become deeper, but without reaching a completely agreed synthesis. I am certainly not expert enough in this field to attempt to do more than indicate some of the factors involved, without trying to bring them into their correct relations with one another. Moreover, for our present purposes, such a synthesis is scarcely necessary. The point I wish to emphasize is that the initial differentiation of the baby's mind into a tripartite system of id, ego and super-ego, with which its development into an ethicizing creature and an authority-accepting creature is intimately bound up, is brought about by very peculiar processes—processes so odd that one could scarcely expect them to bring into being a personality-structure with just an adequate respect for authority and no more. It is no surprise to find Anna Freud writing, in the first place (p. 128): 'True morality begins when the internalized criticism, now embodied in the standard exacted by the super-ego, coincides with the ego's perception of its own faults' and proceeding (p. 59) to point out that the super-ego is 'a redoubtable force. It appears in the light of the author of all neurosis'.

In order to bring home the oddity of these processes, it is worth looking at them rather more closely. In the first place, it will be remembered that Anna Freud considered the main defences of the just-forming ego to be regression, reversal or the turning round upon the self. The first of these is, in fact, a refusal to develop, and cannot be carried very far if the personality is ever to become mature. The second and third involve the diversion of the instinctual drives from their appropriate objects. One could not anticipate that the results of turning instincts for aggressive or sexual behaviour from their external objects on to the self would be simple and straightforward.

Even greater complications are to be expected if projection and introjection play an important part at this very early stage, as they undoubtedly do later. To indicate the type of process indicated by these names, it may be as well to quote some paragraphs from contributions which were made by Karin Stephen and Melanie Klein to the discussion of my original essay on *Science and Ethics* in 1942. (In reading these at the present time, one should remember that we have since realized that an adult's unconscious mind has perhaps as much influence on a child as does his conscious personality.)

Karin Stephen wrote: 'Dr Waddington quotes Mrs Klein as "regarding the impulses of the individual as the fundamental factor in the formation of the super-ego".' What she means here is *not* simply that the child has a nature of its own which reacts with the requirements of its parents and later of society. What is meant is that the child projects its own unacceptable impulses on to the outside world and that it is these very same projected

167

impulses of its own which it re-introjects and sets up inside itself as its super-ego. This means that if, for instance, it experiences primitive impulses of rage or cruelty from which it takes flight because its ego is too weak to manage them, it may be obliged to deal with them instead, by externalizing them, by projection on to its parents, and thus it builds up a fantastic picture (called an imago) of these outside people modelled on its own impulses. This picture will be cruel, murderous and also unmanageable and overpowerful like its own repudiated impulses, and when such an imago is introjected to form the child's own super-ego this will behave ruthlessly and cruelly to its unfortunate victim, just as savagely in fact as the child itself wanted to behave when it experienced the impulses which, in its panic, it was driven to project outside itself. The same vital energies which provided the driving force behind the child's own impulses of cruelty, revenge, murder or whatever it may have been will now re-animate the re-introjected imago which constitutes its tyrannical and cruel super-ego.'

Mrs Klein's description of the process was as follows:

'Here, in brief outline, are some of the facts which have become clear to me in my psychoanalytic work with young children, and which I wish to bring to your notice. The feeling of "good" in the baby's mind, first arises from the experience of *pleasurable* sensations, or, at least, freedom from painful internal and external stimuli. (Food is therefore particularly good, producing, as it does, gratification and relief from discomfort.)[1] Evil is that which causes the baby *pain* and tension, and fails to satisfy his needs and desires. Since the differentiation between "me" and "not-me" hardly exists at the beginning, goodness within and goodness without, badness within and badness without, are almost identical to the child. Soon, however, the conception (though this abstract word does not fit these largely unconscious and highly emotional processes) of "good" and

---

[1] In this sentence Mrs Klein is, in my opinion, using the word 'good' in a non-ethical sense. Ethicizing, I suggest, does not begin until the child starts to react to its parents.

"evil" extends to the actual people around him. The parents also become embued with goodness and badness according to the child's feelings about them, and then are retaken into the ego, and, within the mind, their influence determines the individual conception of good and evil. This movement to and fro between projection and introjection is a continuous process, by which, in the first years of childhood, relationships with actual people are established and the various aspects of the super-ego are at the same time built up within the mind.

'The child's mental capacity to establish people, in the first place his parents, within his own mind, as if they were part of himself, is determined by two facts: on the one hand, stimuli from without and from within, being at first almost undifferentiated, become interchangeable; and on the other, the baby's greed, his wish to take in external good, enhances the process of introjection in such a way that certain experiences of the external world become almost simultaneously part of his inner world.

'The baby's inherent feelings of love as well as of hatred are in the first place focused on his mother. Love develops in response to her love and care; hatred and aggression are stimulated by frustrations and discomfort. At the same time she becomes the object upon whom he projects his *own* emotions. By attributing to his parents his own sadistic tendencies he develops the cruel aspect of his super-ego (as Dr Stephen has already pointed out); but he also projects on to the people around him his feelings of love, and by these means develops the image of kind and helpful parents. From the first day of life, these processes are influenced by the actual attitudes of the people who look after him, and experiences of the actual outer world and inner experiences constantly interact. In endowing his parents with his feelings of love and thus building up the later ego-ideal, the child is driven by imperative physical and mental needs; he would perish without his mother's food and care, and his whole mental well-being and development depend on his establishing securely in his mind the existence of kind and protective figures.

'The various aspects of the super-ego derive from the way in which, throughout successive stages of development, the child conceives of his parents. Another powerful element in the formation of the super-ego is the child's own feelings of revulsion against his own aggressive tendencies—a revulsion which he experiences unconsciously as early as in the first few months of life. How are we to explain this early turning of one part of the mind against the other—this inherent tendency to self-condemnation, which is the root of conscience? One imperative motive can be found in the unconscious fear of the child, in whose mind desires and feelings are omnipotent, that should his violent impulses prevail, they would bring about the destruction both of his parents and of himself, since the parents in his mind have become an integral part of his self (super-ego).

'The child's overwhelming fear of losing the people he loves and most needs initiates in his mind not only the impulse to restrain his aggression but also a drive to preserve the very objects whom he attacks in phantasy, to put them right and to make amends for the injuries he may have inflicted on them. This drive to make reparation adds impetus and direction to the creative impulse and to all constructive activities. Something is now added to the early conception of good and evil: "Good" becomes the preserving, repairing or re-creating of those objects which are endangered by his hatred or have been injured by it. "Evil" becomes his own dangerous hatred.

'Constructive and creative activities, social and co-operative feelings, are then felt to be morally good, and they are therefore the most important means of keeping at bay or overcoming the sense of guilt. When the various aspects of the super-ego have become unified (which is the case with mature and well-balanced people), the feeling of guilt has not been put out of action, but has become, together with the means of counteracting it, integrated in the personality. If guilt is too strong and cannot be dealt with adequately, it may lead to actions which create more guilt still (as in the criminal) and become the cause for abnormal development of all kinds.'

It is unnecessary here to pursue further the various theories which psychoanalysts have advanced concerning the initial stages in the differentiation of the personality into its three major systems. Nor do we need to follow the course of this differentiation into the periods of latency and adolescence, with which the ego-psychology of today is so largely concerned. Enough has been said to make the point that the newborn child becomes an ethicizing creature by means of some very odd processes. Some development of 'authority-bearing systems' is, as we have said, necessary to mould the baby into an information-acceptor; and the formation of such systems is found in fact also to involve his becoming a being which 'goes in for ethics'. What emerges, if the psychoanalysts are even partially justified in their account of the matter, is that the processes which the human species has evolved for bringing about this result are of a kind which will almost inevitably lead to an over-development of authority. The super-ego is, in Anna Freud's words, the 'author of all neurosis'. Even if we confine our attention to the conscious part of the mind, it is a remarkable fact—and presumably a consequence of the same peculiarity of these early processes of differentiation— that we tend to demand of our ethical beliefs a degree of certainty which we would never look for in any other doctrines. They should, we feel, be universal in scope, absolute in character, and unassailable in validity.

I suggested[1] that ethical systems tend to have their characteristic tone of other-worldliness and absoluteness partly because the events which precipitate their formation are exactly those which first break down the solipsistic state of 'harmonious mixed-up-ness' in which we exist in the first few weeks of life. Balint has discussed the importance of the loss of this state of primitive harmony for the development of the idea of external objects as something totally separate and removed from ourselves. 'Our very first perceptions about objects,' he writes, 'may be those of resistance, i.e. something firm against which we may pit our strength, either successfully or unsuccessfully.' The point I am making about the development of authority is essentially similar. Some of our very first experiences are those of an authority which says 'No', something which resists or denies our wishes. Such experiences are aggravating enough at the best of times;

[1] 1942.

171

intruding into a state in which we had not yet reached the stage of distinguishing between ourselves and the external world they must indeed be traumatic.

I should not wish to claim that the break-up of a solipsistic state was the only influence at work in endowing the internal personalized authorities with their *quasi* absolute quality. When my original essay was first published, another factor in the situation was pointed out by Dr Julian Huxley. This 'concerns the basis for the quality of absoluteness and other worldliness possessed by the super-ego and the systems of ethics for which it is the vehicle. Dr Waddington makes what I believe to be the quite novel suggestion that this is connected with the breakdown of the solipsistic early phase of the child's existence. While this may be a contributory cause of the other worldliness, I cannot feel that it accounts for the absoluteness, for the fact that certain aspects of morality are felt as a categorical imperative. The origin of this, as I have elsewhere suggested, must more probably be sought in the all-or-nothing method adopted in higher animals for avoiding conflict. This has been proved to operate to prevent conflict between antagonistic muscles and between competing reflexes. Observation shows that it must also normally apply to competing instincts in sub-human vertebrates. Finally, all we know of human psychology indicates the strong probability that it operates in repression in early life. Man is the only organism in which conflict is normal and habitual, so that some form for minimizing its effects is essential; and this will be of the greatest importance in early childhood, before sufficient experience has been accumulated to enable conflict to be dealt with empirically and rationally.

'The antagonistic forces which hold down repressed ideas and impulses are kept away from the main body of consciousness; hence the apparent externality of ethical law. They are held there by the strong but automatic processes of repression; hence the compulsiveness of the super-ego. And repression is, or attempts to be, total, seeking to keep certain impulses wholly out of consciousness; hence the all-or-nothing character of the ethical prohibitions of the super-ego.'

It is clear that the processes of repression to which Huxley refers, and the breakdown of solipsism, which I have mentioned, are not in any way exclusive of one another, but may both proceed simultaneously. What I think emerges from all these discussions is that the processes which we have reason to believe are going on in the first few weeks of life are sufficiently extraordinary to be responsible for producing ethical authorities which have the qualities of other-worldliness and absoluteness that we find in our ethical feelings, as well as the guilt and anxiety which are another of their unexpected but obtrusive characteristics. We find ourselves coming back, from a somewhat unexpected direction, to the old apprehension of mankind that eating the fruit of the Tree of Knowledge (functioning as an information-acceptor) is essentially connected with the knowledge of good and evil, that is, becoming an ethicizing being; and connected also with a sense of sin (guilt and anxiety) and finally with a feeling of a need for a super-natural authority.

In my original exposition, I was mainly concerned to make the point—which I think had not been made before—that the existence of ethical beliefs is a necessary part of the human evolutionary system. Pursuing this line of thought I emphasized the conclusion that if this is the case, we can assign a function to the existence of ethical beliefs, and can therefore utilize the efficiency with which this function is fulfilled as a criterion for deciding between alternative systems of belief which we may encounter. In emphasizing this argument, which I still regard as the most important thesis advanced, I laid little stress on the already well-recognized point that it is desirable to reduce as far as possible the harmful and unpleasant consequences which follow from the peculiar manner in which the authority-systems become set up. I discussed the odd events of projection and introjection, of the breakdown of solipsism, and so on, almost entirely from the point of view of attempting to account for such peculiar qualities as absoluteness which characterize ethical beliefs and which seem to require a special explanation; but several of those who discussed the original thesis pointed out that the amelioration or the taming of the super-ego is one of the aims which man ought to set before himself. Thus Huxley,[1] after comparing my ideas

[1] 1947, p. 187.

with the Marxist formulation of ethics, writes as follows: 'It is true that the Marxists assert that morality is an organ of one class within society, while Waddington would make it an organ of society as a whole; but in both cases it is regarded merely as a social organ, whose function is to secure the persistence and success of a social group. On the contrary, I would maintain that morality has also an individual function, negatively in liberating the individual from some at least of his load of guilt, and positively in guiding him towards what the Bible calls righteousness —ethical fulfilment, the achievement of moral nobility of personality, a sense of oneness with something beyond and larger than ourselves, which is itself either moral or transcends and includes morality.' And Dr Karin Stephen wrote (pp. 59–60): 'I agree with Professor Huxley that domination by a blind and autocratic super-ego, deadlocking with the energies or vital impulses, is destructive to the human personality, and that its modification of this mechanistic type of self-regulation would produce "good". . . . The theory underlying the view of good and evil to which we both subscribe seems to be that the subject matter of ethics is human personalities: evil would coincide roughly with neurosis and psychosis, i.e. with mental and moral disease, and good with spiritual growth, health and sanity.'

I am certainly ready to agree that my original statement placed less emphasis on this aspect of the matter than it deserves. In an earlier chapter of this book I have discussed extensively the evolution of evolutionary systems. If, as I maintain, our ethical beliefs are part of the human evolutionary system, they also must be subject to evolutionary processes. Since we can discern their function, we can decide what is anagenesis with respect to them, just as we can decide what is anagenesis with respect to the biological genetic system. We can attach a real and objective meaning to the idea of an improvement in the mechanism of formation and development of the super-ego as a part of the functional machinery of human evolution. This direction of improvement undoubtedly forms one of the criteria which we must apply in judging the merits of particular ethical systems.

CHAPTER 14

Freedom and Reason

IN recent years the centre of progress in our understanding of biological evolution has been in the United States, where there has been an exceptionally active group of workers, such as Dobzhansky, Simpson, Mayr, Stebbins and others, who have shown a depth of knowledge and breadth of outlook which demands that they be regarded as something more than mere biological specialists. Several of them have discussed the relation between evolution and ethics, and their views must be treated with the greatest respect. The two main discussions which require consideration are those given by Dobzhansky and G. G. Simpson.

Both authors discuss first the various theories, such as the 'Ethico-genesis' of Leake, which are concerned with the processes by which genes might be selected which favour the development of altruistic behaviour. They agree with the conclusion reached above (p. 25) that this problem, though an interesting one, does not provide a basis for understanding the nature of the moral sense, or any criterion by which moral systems can be evaluated. Both then proceed further to the discussion of theories of ethics of the same general character as I have been advancing. However, although Dobzhansky, though not Simpson, gives a reference to my *Science and Ethics*, they base their discussion primarily on the form in which the theory emerged when it was treated by Julian Huxley in his *Evolution and Ethics*. Thus they appreciate and agree with the notion that social transmission provides the human species with a new mechanism of evolution, but they have not apparently taken the point that it is suggested that ethicizing is inextricably bound up with the processes by which a newborn human being becomes moulded into a receiver of culturally-transmitted information. In so far as they fail to grasp this point they remain unaware of what seems to me the essential link by which the field of ethical concepts is connected with the ideas of evolution.

Dobzhansky writes (p. 128): 'No theory of evolutionary ethics can be acceptable unless it gives a satisfactory explanation of just why the promotion of evolutionary development must be regarded as the *summum bonum*. . . . Despite any exhortations to the contrary, man will not permanently deny himself the right to question the wisdom of anything, including the wisdom of his evolutionary direction.' In writing this, Dobzhansky was presumably using the word 'wisdom' in a rather general sense, and not with the special connotation with which I have employed it here. When used without previous indication of a particular meaning, the word may be taken in several different senses. From the general tenor of the discussion, one suspects that the meaning which was uppermost in Dobzhansky's mind was one in which 'wisdom' was more or less equivalent to 'goodness', so that his criticism becomes equivalent to the usual argument of philosophers against the naturalistic fallacy, as it has been set forth, for instance, by Moore (p. 51). An answer to this has already been given: what I am trying to do is not to formulate another description by which goodness can be recognized, but a criterion by which beliefs concerning the nature of goodness can be judged; and I have pointed out that such a criterion for judgement of a different logical status to the notion of goodness itself. I suggested that the word 'wisdom' might be used in a restricted sense to refer to a criterion of this kind. If one were to interpret the 'wisdom' in Dobzhansky's sentence in this restricted manner, his remarks would, I think, no longer amount to a criticism. In this narrow sense I have defined 'wisdom' as a belief which fulfils sufficiently the function of mediating evolutionary advance. One could, therefore, not question the wisdom of evolutionary advance since that is a matter of definition. One could continue to question the wisdom of anything else, but if the word is being used in this sense, the definition of it provides a method by which one could answer the question.

These two interpretations of Dobzhansky's 'wisdom' probably do not exhaust the content which he reposed in it. He continues the sentences quoted above as follows: 'He (man) may rebel against this direction (of evolution), even though it may be shown to be a beneficial one. Just such an "unreasonable" rebellion was envisaged by Dostoievesky in his *Letters from the Underworld*. Man is likely to prefer to be free rather than to be reasonable. As Simpson put it: "There is no ethics but human ethics and a search that ignores the necessity that ethics be human, relative to man, is bound to fail." ' The quotation from Simpson comes from his *The Meaning of Evolution* (p. 307), and a reading of this gives a little more clarity to the at first rather obscure point of what Simpson means by 'the necessity that ethics be human'. It seems that, like Dobzhansky, he is emphasizing that the ethically good is something that man must *choose* to do. Naturalistic ethics, he writes, 'still try to find an external standard, one given without need for choice and without other requirements than discovery and acceptance. . . . The point is that an *evolutionary ethics for man* (which is of course the one we, as men, seek, if not the only possible kind) should be based on man's own nature, on his evolutionary position and significance. It cannot be expected to arise *automatically* from the principles of evolution in general, nor yet, indeed, from those of human evolution in particular. It cannot be expected to be absolute, but must be subject to evolution itself and must be the result of responsible and rational *choice* in the full light of such knowledge of man and of life as we have.'

There seems to be three things to be said about this insistence on the importance of choice. The first, which is perhaps rather trivial, is to point out that any general theory of ethics, either of the kinds which have been usual in the philosophy of the past or in the form of a general criterion for evaluating ethical systems such as is suggested here, aims only at providing a framework in which rational discussion is possible. It is not intended to answer all moral questions, but only to guide the directions in which they can be discussed. Ample scope is left for rational choice, that is to say for the decision between alternatives on grounds which can be stated and argued about. It is, however, probably not rational decision between alternatives that Dobzhansky and Simpson had in mind. Dobzhansky's words

177

in particular, and his reference to Dostoievsky, would suggest that he had in mind the profound contrariness of human nature. We all know that man has a deep-seated tendency to refuse to do what his reason tells him, in fact to reject a course of action partly at least just because all the staid and solid arguments seem to be on its side. But this tendency surely cannot be taken as a guide to the conclusions which rational philosophical thought should reach. If it were no conclusions would be possible. Just as they were approached, the demand for freedom in this sense would upset the applecart. Moreover, we now know, largely owing to the discoveries of psychoanalysis in the broad sense, a great deal more about these internal revolts against the dictates of reason. They seem to arise, as is discussed in more detail in Chapter 10, from the peculiarities of the process by which authoritative systems are set up in the mind. We can regard them not merely as something given in innate human nature, but as unconscious tendencies concerning which we have an inkling of a dynamic understanding, which can be discussed, vaguely and tentatively it is true, in terms of such concepts as the super-ego, the id and so on. Certainly our understanding of them is very incomplete, and we can probably at present go no further than the psychoanalysts' ideal of the formation of what they call a 'healthy mind', an ideal which they formulate in terms of the absorption of as much as possible of the super-ego and id into the ego. Dobzhansky introduces into his discussion the word free, a notoriously difficult notion to understand. One of its meanings is that which makes reasonable the well-known statement that freedom is the knowledge of necessity. In my opinion, the employment of reason in human affairs, and the formulation of criteria by which rational evaluations can be made between alternatives, increases rather than decreases man's freedom in the most important sense of that word. I therefore cannot accept the view which Dobzhansky and Simpson may be taken to suggest, that a rational criterion for ethics cannot be acceptable because it limits the essential human faculty for the exercise of freedom.

There is, however, still another way in which Dobzhansky and Simpson's words can be taken. The whole treatment of ethics in this book has remained within the sphere of rational verbal discussion. Its aim, like that of most recent Western philosophy, has been to produce conceptual hypotheses which can be argued about. The best it could hope to achieve would be logical consistency and factual plausibility within that type of thought. But there is a completely different mode of approach to the whole subject, one which is not a criticism of rationalist theories, since it does not lie within the sphere of conceptual thought, but is rather complementary to it. I referred to this somewhat hesitantly and half-heartedly in the original discussion of this argument, and quoted in the concluding remarks (*Science and Ethics*, p. 139), William Blake's aphorisms 'General good is the plea of the scoundrel, hypocrite and flatterer. . . . To generalize is to be an idiot. . . . He who would do good to another must do it in minute particulars.' These quotations, however, do not perhaps quite explicitly make the point, which would perhaps better have been conveyed by a reference to St Francis of Assissi.

There are, I mean, certain people who seem to be naturally good, without effort and certainly without any rationally formulated system of ethical thought or judgment. Taking such people as a model, one can approach the subject of ethics with the aim of reaching a state in which good action is as spontaneous and unthinking as the heartbeat or the movement of the lungs in respiration. There are several oriental philosophies which have followed this path, and there has recently been considerably increased interest in them in the West. One of the most general of these movements is Chinese Taoism. An inkling of its attitude can be conveyed by a quotation from Lao-Tzu[1]:

> Cut out sagacity; discard knowingness,
> And the people will benefit an hundredfold.
> Cut out 'humanity'; discard righteousness,
> And the people will regain love of their fellows.
> Cut out cleverness; discard the utilitarian,
> And there will be no thieves and robbers. . . .
> Become unaffected;

[1] Translated in Watts, 1959a.

179

Cherish sincerity;
Belittle the personal;
Reduce desires.

Watts goes on: 'The idea is not to reduce the human mind to a moronic vacuity, but to bring into play its innate and spontaneous intelligence by using it without forcing it.' Again, in another pamphlet,[1] Watts gives a quotation from the writings of the Japanese school of Zen philosophy:

If you want to get the plain truth,
Be not concerned with right and wrong.
The conflict between right and wrong
Is the sickness of the mind.

It seems rather likely that when Dobzhansky and Simpson were referring to freedom and choice, and the necessity for ethics to be truly human, one of the notions in their mind was allied to this concept of total spontaneity and naturalness. I should certainly have no wish to minimize the value of this type of approach to ethical problems, but it is, I think, on a different plane to that of rational thought, and does not really impinge on, let alone contradict, any conceptual philosophical theory. This conclusion, that both types of approach have their own validity, is also to be found in the adherents of Taoist or Zen thought. For instance, Watts, after quoting the four lines given above, goes on as follows: 'But this standpoint does not exclude and is not hostile towards the distinction between right and wrong at other levels, and in more limited frames of reference. The world is seen to be beyond right and wrong when it is not framed; that is to say, when we are not looking at a particular situation by itself—out of relation to the rest of the universe. Within this room there is a clear distinction between up and down; out in inter-stellar space, there is not. Within the conventional limits of a human community there are clear distinctions between good and evil. But these disappear when human affairs are seen as part and parcel of the whole realm of nature.'

[1] 1959b.

180

The point which is most profound and valuable in the comments of Dobzhansky and Simpson is not one which, in my opinion, invalidates the attempt to formulate, on the basis of our understanding of evolutionary processes, a rational framework within which ethical problems can be discussed. These two writers are not only deeply learned biologists who have added greatly to our understanding of evolution, but are profound human beings. They may of course be right and I be wrong, within the sphere of conceptual rational discourse in which I have rejected their criticism, but whichever of us is adjudged correct there, their words raise another type of consideration which is extremely important although falling outside the type of mental activity on which this book is based.

These oriental philosophies are only examples, although at present rather fashionable ones in western Europe and America, of a wide range of types of thought which lay emphasis on the importance of human freedom or choice, and which represent this as something which has to be apprehended in a mystical or at least in a non-rational manner. Having said so much in acknowledgment of their value, it may not be out of order to indicate what seem to be their weaknesses in relation to modern ethical problems. Nearly all such forms of thought pay insufficient attention to the fact that a fully-developed human being is inconceivable in isolation from society. Human individuality only arises within a social framework, and its maturation depends essentially on the social means of communication, that is to say, conceptual thought and language. An attempt to do without intellectual thought, and to handle the affairs of life 'naturally' and 'spontaneously' as we move our bodies in walking, must, if pushed too far, lead to the abolition of one of the most important elements in human nature. The use of reason is as natural to us as our heartbeat. A satisfactory 'way of life' has to comprise them both.

The situations which today confront us with the most important ethical problems have in fact largely been created by the application of intellectual thought. As has been pointed out several times already, they are matters of social policy affecting large populations of people. In the mode of thought which passes directly from the isolated individual to the general nature of the universe, this stratum of affairs is often almost completely omitted. Systems like the Tao and Zen have in fact usually existed as a conscious opposition force within societies which were dominated by highly organized systems of government, which dealt with the practical affairs of society in general. The source-book of Taoism by Lao-Tzu does indeed contain advice about how social affairs should be looked after, but the points it makes would be valuable only as mitigations of a system which was already efficient, though perhaps too stringent; they do little to indicate how effective courses of action are to be found. For instance, we read (in the translation by Witter Bynner):

> Handle a large kingdom with as gentle a touch as
>   if you were cooking small fish.
> If you manage people by letting them alone,
> Ghosts of the dead shall not haunt you.

Or again, the very valuable but still partial advice:

> A leader is best
> When people barely know that he exists,
> Not so good when people obey and acclaim him,
> Worst when they despise him.
> Fail to honour people,
> They fail to honour you;
> But of a good leader, who talks little,
> When his work is done, his aim fulfilled,
> They will all say, 'We did this ourselves.'

Very true, but just how is the leader or the people to decide what is to be done? Surely, we shall not be more true to our human nature but less, if, in deciding on courses of action, we neglect our main human apparatus for handling such matters, namely, conceptual thought; and when the problems to be solved have been set by the application of intellectual analysis, the need for rationality in dealing with them is all the more obvious.

CHAPTER 15

Understanding and Believing

EVEN though it may appear very unwise to shirk the task of pushing our rational understanding of the human situation as far as we can take it, the simplest empirical observation is all that is necessary to convince one that there are other aspects of man's mental life which cannot be left out of account. Throughout the whole period of European civilization which, one is almost constrained to say, has just ended, matters of belief have been the central focus around which human life has orientated itself. We regard ourselves as the heirs of a Christian civilization, and for centuries it was accepted without question that the fundamental cultural boundary was between the Believers and the Heathen. Within each realm, the differences which divided men into more or less exclusive and often hostile groups were usually expressed in terms of belief in certain formulated doctrines. Some of the most ferocious of all wars have raged between people who considered that their most important characteristic was a belief in Catholicism or Protestantism, in the Divine Right of Kings, in Liberty, Equality and Fraternity, or some other such ideal.

Many modern historians would wish to look behind the dividing lines drawn in terms of belief, and claim that one can discover other factors, usually economic in the broad sense, which separated the various groups, and of which, they argue, the consciously held beliefs were mere rationalizations couched in the fashionable religious terminology of the age. That may well be largely true; but it must still be recognized that, as far as an individual man attempted to control his own behaviour, and act as a conscious agent, it was by such beliefs that he was influenced. The religious martyrs did not, consciously, die on behalf of a rising class of entrepreneurs or bourgeois middle-

183

men, but for points of doctrine. And even those who did not in fact believe anything deeply enough to die for it, seem for the most part to have considered beliefs as things to which it was quite proper to give such attachment, were not everyday human nature all too weak for such devotion.

In speaking of beliefs in this way, I am not, of course, referring to comparatively trivial theories concerned with the details of behaviour. A man may believe in the wisdom of the editors of his daily newspaper, in the existence of ghosts, or the value of boarding schools for boys, for any of a number of reasons, most of which are likely to be related to the satisfaction of his conscious or unconscious wishes. Such convictions are not of the first importance even for moulding the believer's own character, let alone for the history of civilization. But a much greater importance must be attached to the ultimate general beliefs or fundamental ideals which provide the guiding principle on which men try, somewhat intermittently perhaps, to direct their lives, and which are the aspiration towards which they feel they ought to strive. It is these major ideals—such things as Christianity, Reason or Communism—that I shall be referring to when I speak of beliefs.

A simple inspection of the behaviour of one's fellows is adequate evidence that even if a man gives as accurate a statement of what he believes as he is capable of formulating, that provides only a very rough and incomplete guide to his character. And at a more critical level of study, psychoanalysts have shown conclusively that consciously held beliefs form only a small part of a much larger complex in the mental structure. Much of this complex normally remains below the level of consciousness, as the greater part of an iceberg is beneath the surface of the sea. Exactly which part floats uppermost, and comes within our vision, is partly a matter of chance. Although there are certain elements of the complex whose nature is such that they tend to be more accessible, the ideas with which these parts become clothed are subject to two sorts of variation, due on the one hand to the nature of the deeper levels on which they are based, and on the other to the particular, rather arbitrarily chosen symbols by which the nature of those levels happen to be expressed in the individual concerned.

The wealth of evidence which modern psychologists, and particularly psychoanalysts, have presented on these matters is such that the intellectual world has been persuaded, for the last twenty years or so, of the general truth of their conclusions, at least in broad outline. Applying such an outlook to one's own thought, as one must, one has to concede that no belief, however firmly held, and no axiom, however self-evident, can provide a basis for deductions about the objective world. The essential conclusion was stated quite clearly by Ernest Jones in the first of his papers on psychoanalysis in a book published over thirty years ago, '. . . whenever an individual considers a given (mental) process as being too obvious to permit of any investigation into its origin, and shows resistance to such an investigation, we are right in suspecting that the actual origin is concealed from him—almost certainly on account of its unacceptable nature. Reflection shows that this criterion applies to an enormous number of our fixed beliefs—religious, ethical, political and hygienic, as well as to a great part of our daily conduct; in other words, the principle above quoted refers to a large sphere of mental processes where we least suspect it.' At the time they were written, those sentences must have seemed at best doubtful to most people, and frank heresy to many; today the idea they contain should be one of the central methodological principles in all enquiry into the relations between human beliefs and human behaviour, or between metaphysical systems and the objective world.

It is easy to deduce from such a principle that it is vain to search, as philosophers and metaphysicians and moralists have done for so long, after final truths which may be accepted without question and used as the foundations on which a whole system of thought may be erected. Many philosophers, of course, had already come to a similar conclusion on other grounds. Plato, for instance, states somewhere that the highest truths cannot be expressed as doctrines, but only as myths. And in our own times, Whitehead[1] has insisted that 'philosophy is akin to poetry, and both of them seek to express that ultimate good

[1] 1938, p. 238.

sense which we term civilization'. But in recent years the re-
pudiation by philosophers of the task of formulating anything
worthy of even a shadow of belief has gone much further. The
Logical Positivists argued that no meaning can be attached to
any statement which is not either an assertion of bare fact or a
proposition of logic; and their linguistic successors make it their
proudest boast that their work does not impinge on beliefs or
ways of seeing the world, but 'leaves everything as it is'.

The course of recent history has, however, provided a terrify-
ing exposure of the unacceptableness of a call for scepticism, and
the dangers of a high-minded silence about human beliefs. For
civilization has obviously been caught on both horns of a
dilemma. While, on the one side, the intellectual basis for the
acceptance of any form of belief has been undermined, on the
other, our political development has been distorted by the profound influence of new myths, which have attracted to themselves
more fanatical devotion than any other set of beliefs for the last
century or more. It is the oldest, most thoroughly tested beliefs
which have been given up; not only the ancient elaborately
rationalized doctrines such as Christianity, but also the less precisely formulated ideals, such as humanitarianism, liberalism,
neighbourliness, which were so influential during the last few
centuries. But the place of the former theologies has been taken,
and more than filled, by new doctrinal schemes such as Communism, free enterprise, the various brands of national socialism,
and the cruder nationalisms which are qualified by little or no
social aim; while the older values have been replaced by such
ideals as efficiency, ruthlessness in attaining a desired end,
equalitarianism, or the leadership principle, and whole hosts of
others.

I have no wish to claim that all these doctrines or ideals are
necessarily unworthy of devotion. Among them are to be found
the forces that will shape the future, and, speaking for myself, I
can see, clearly enough to feel a moderate optimism, potentialities for a future far preferable to the past. The only point I wish
to make here is that these newer doctrines and beliefs, the good
and the bad alike, have called forth an intensity of belief which
is in flat contradiction to the understanding which we now have

of how beliefs are formed and the reasons for which they are held.

There is no need to labour the point and quote more examples. We see clearly that the preliminary analysis of the nature of belief carried out in the early years of the century, has had consequences of both a negative and a positive kind—negative in that it loosened the hold of the older creeds, and positive by the rather indirect route that it was in actual fact followed by the adoption of a large variety of new doctrines, many of which at least pretended to be 'scientific'. This evidence is enough to warn us that it is inadequate to draw from the recent analysis merely the pious aspiration that men's conduct should not be affected by any tenet which cannot be proved by the objective criteria of science. There is no doubt that all men's actions (including, let us remember, our own) will continue to be profoundly influenced by beliefs which are held for quite other reasons than the weight of the evidence which supports them.

The wars, tortures, forced migrations and other calculated brutalities which make up so much of recent history, have for the most part been carried out by men who earnestly believed that their actions were justified, and, indeed, demanded, by the application of certain basic principles in which they believed. Such events provide, surely, proof enough that the belief-structure, whose function is essentially that of restraining the aboriginal id, has a crude power which may lead it to act quite unlike a gentlemanly and kind policeman. This hypertrophy of the human control mechanism, which was discussed in Chapter 13, is rather surprising. It may be that the primitive urges are so strong, and would, if left to themselves, be so incompatible with social existence that a dangerously powerful belief-structure is indispensable before man can reap any evolutionary advantage from living in groups. But it may also be asked whether our present development of the super-ego does not represent an over-specialization, comparable to the excessive body-armour of the later dinosaurs, or the finicky adaptation of certain parasites which fits them to live on only one host. It would be interesting to know whether the differentiation of the human mind into opposing factions— roughly speaking, into id and super-ego—has increased in

187

modern civilized man as compared with the primitive savages of the still existing Stone Age cultures. Is the apparent prevalence of neurosis in Western civilization a mere consequence of better diagnosis, or the result of the greater strain of industrial civilization, or due to a real over-specialization in the direction of human evolution? If the latter suggestion is true, then the self-destruction of mankind in wars of political religion, which hangs as such an obvious threat over our heads, will be merely one more example in the long tale of evolutionary doom following on over-specialization.

We may find some encouragement in the reflection that present biological theory supposes that most new major steps in evolution, such as the origin of a new phylum, happened as a result of an efflorescence of exaggerated and almost uncontrolled variation, which finally threw up some novel but harmonious type of organization. Perhaps we can regard mankind as only in the outlandish but formative phase through which a more durably satisfactory socio-genetic system will be attained.

The potential destructiveness of our beliefs has, of course, been recognized by many students of these matters. It has not been easy to prescribe an antidote. Some have been tempted to suggest a very radical remedy. For instance, in a recent lecture, General Chisholm, a distinguished psychiatrist who was Director-General of Medical Services in the Canadian Army, and then Executive Secretary of the World Health Organization of the United Nations, went so far as to suggest that we should abolish beliefs, 'stop teaching children moralities and rights and wrong, . . . the poison long ago described and warned against as the fruit of the tree of the knowledge of good and evil'. Instead we should 'protect their original intellectual integrity'. But can we find an original integrity which is independent of the belief-structure mechanism of organizing social life? If I have been on the right lines in the previous discussion, in which I have argued that the setting up of a system of ideals in opposition to the primitive urges is the essential feature of a new evolutionary method, then we cannot merely abolish one-half of the dualism, however hypertorphied it may have become.

We need to approach the matter more cautiously and to devote more careful study to the exact nature of the system which we wish to control. What, then, are the broad structural features of that complex of beliefs and their unconscious counterparts which exercises a restraining and directing function within the human mind? And further, since we cannot contemplate the abolition of this complex, we need to enquire what types of internal balance may be set up within such complexes as enable their possessors to live active, creative and co-operative lives. A very great deal more thorough and professional study must still be devoted to such questions. We can as yet give only incomplete and very tentative answers.

We may take it that the main element in a belief-structure is the representative of authority. Ultimately this may be regarded as the introjection of a parent or parent-substitute, but in the shifting alchemy of the developing personality, the original human authority may come to be symbolized by many different images and ideas. The function of this element in the complex is to restrain and direct the energies of the primitive physiological urges, and it can only do this by virtue of a measure of love, reverence and submission which is paid to it by the remainder of the self. But this submission cannot be absolute; the primitive urges, and the id which represents them, struggle against restraint; the belief-structure is the subject of hate as well as of love. This sets up a conflict. As Anna Freud has shown, it is possible, and indeed enlightening, to regard the whole structure of the psyche in terms of the defences utilized by the ego to counter the attacks of the id and super-ego (and of the external world).

Now, as we well know in other situations, phenomena which are at all closely comparable to attack and defence may, sometimes, come to a balanced equilibrium which remains comparatively stable, but they often do not. The anthropologist Bateson has, perhaps, gone as far as anyone in systematizing our understanding of the ways in which conflict situations between individuals or groups of people may develop. He coined the word *schismogenesis* to mean 'a process of differentiation in the norms of individual behaviour resulting from the cumulative interaction between individuals'; and in his original discussion of the matter expressly raised the possibility that an essentially similar process may occur between different aspects of the same mind.[1] Bateson originally distinguished two types of schismogenesis, complementary and symmetrical. In the former, the two actors in the situation behave in opposite ways to one another; A, for instance, may be aggressive towards B, who responds by being submissive. The symmetrical configuration arises when both act similarly; A perhaps boasting to B, who boasts back. Both types of interaction tend to result in progressive change, which, if uncontrolled, leads to the destruction of the system.

One must therefore ask, what type of control is possible? Bateson originally suggested only that, in functioning societies, a certain intensity of symmetrical behaviour happened to balance with an appropriate degree of complementariness. In the Epilogue which he wrote for the second edition of *Naven*, he is able to go further, and to show that the essential feature of satisfactory control is that there should be a functional relationship or 'communication channel' which ensures that 'an increase in symmetrical schismogenesis will bring about an increase in the corrective complementary phenomena'. For instance, if A boasts too much, B must be brought by this to stop his competitive boasting, and, perhaps become receptive or sceptical.

Before considering the application of these ideas to conflicts within a single mind, there is another point to be brought out. When the feedbacks in the system lead one member of a schismogenic situation to break off from his previous complementary or symmetrical behaviour *vis-a-vis* the other member, it very frequently happens that not only is the pattern of behaviour changed, but, we may say, a change of subject occurs. A and B compete in boasting till, say, B stops boasting and behaves in some other way—perhaps by becoming aggressive, to which A responds, not by more boasting but by beginning to be submissive. We have not a mere alternation between symmetrical and complementary behaviour within one context, but a change of context. Something rather parallel to this is seen in the 'displacement activities' described by students of animal behaviour.

Although I have certainly no pretensions to be an expert on

[1] Bateson, 1958, p. 182.

the cybernetic engineering of the human psyche—the building up of suitable self-compensating feedbacks to control the various types of schismogenesis, which is, I suppose, one of the main preoccupations of psychiatrists—it does seem worth drawing attention to the potential importance of change of subject as a controlling factor, since this does not seem to be very often discussed. The essential mechanism is, perhaps, little more than what lay behind the old family doctor's prescription of 'a change of scene'. But it may be particularly important in the context of belief-structures. I think many people, not especially expert in psychology, have a feeling, which I suspect is rather well justified, that a philosophical discussion which leads to just one precise conclusive belief is to be regarded with some caution.

Bateson,[1] in a recent lecture, took as his motto a remark of William Blake:

> . . . May God us Keep
> From Single vision and Newton's Sleep!

Although the context in which he used this was slightly different, the point is the same as that which I am now making. If the love of one ideal leads to some degree of attachment to a second ideal, which, while not the diametrical opposite of the first, is yet of a quite different and contrasting kind to it, then the hate directed at the primary symbol can become mutated into the service of the secondary. To give an example, the Christian belief-structure, which lasted for so long, and for much of this period facilitated the growth of a progressive and fairly stable civilization, involved the two ideals of holy humility and the organized Church: St Francis and the Popes. There was a channel of communication, not easy to close off completely, between the primary attachment to the authority of the Church and the very different ideal of brotherly love which the institution was supposed to serve; and the internal forces of hate directed against the organization could take the form of a devotion to this essentially anarchic aspiration. Again, on a somewhat lower level, the pre-eminently stable British political system has been based on

[1] 1959.

an acceptance of a social hierarchy, mitigated by a devotion to the principle of equal justice for all men. On the other hand, everyone can see at present the dangers to the whole of civilized life which threaten from an exclusive belief in the virtues of 'free enterprise' or in the cause of social organization.

It has, I think, been usual to consider that in a balanced duality of loyalties, the two elements must be of the same nature though opposite in tendency. That is to say, that a belief in the virtues of social organization, for instance, must be countered by a belief in its exact opposite, namely, in social freedom; or a belief in a doctrinaire and hierarchical Church balanced against a belief in the value of the individual conscience. I believe this to be a misinterpretation. A stable mental equilibrium seems to me to be something other than a mere compromise between opposites. It seems rather to involve a relation between entities of different order. The values of the Sermon on the Mount belong to a different sphere to those of the organized Church; and the balance weight to a belief in social organization is to be found, not in the absence of regulations and planning, but in an insistence on the richness and depth of individual experience. Moreover it is not at all necessary that the system should be a dualism, involving only two contrasting components. The essential point is that the personality should have available to it more than a single focus of interest; it should be able to change the subject when necessary. A multi-faceted being may have an even greater factor of safety of this kind than one founded on a dualism.

The individual hate directed against the super-ego probably cannot be simply transmuted into love for its opposite, but can, it appears, take the form (analogous to a 'displacement activity?') of an attachment to some ideal totally other to the primary one. I shall not attempt to discuss possible reasons for this, being certainly unqualified to do so; but they must surely be connected with the relations between the conscious and unconscious parts of the mind, and dependent on the difficulty of accommodating within the one field of consciousness two tenets which are clearly opposite to one another. In general, it must be said here, that the extremely simplified sketch which I am offering of the structure of the belief-function of the mind requires supplementing by a much fuller consideration of the mechanism of repression, which introduces still another dualism, that between the conscious and unconscious representatives of the primitive urges and the restraining authority.

The practical conclusion to be drawn from this line of thought is that it is dangerous to allow questions of belief to become concentrated into a single channel. We have to recognize not merely that it is impossible to eliminate beliefs from the human mind, but that a stable and equable personality must be founded, not only on one, but on several ideals. If we see all things in terms of one shibboleth, in monotone, we shall almost certainly come to see them in stark contrasting opposites, in black and white. We need a multi-dimensional view of the universe.

This conclusion amounts to a denial of the practical value of the philosophers' age-long attempts to reduce the apparent chaos of immediate experience to a single unified and harmonious system of concepts. Of course, in so far as a metaphysical system remains a purely intellectual construction, it does not require criticism on the grounds I have been bringing forward. It would be at least an innocuous component of the mental structure and might even be a useful framework of abstract thought. But so soon as it becomes employed as a guide for action, a metaphysical system must attract to itself some degree of belief; and if, being a comprehensive system, it is taken as the sole guide, it becomes the vehicle for a monotone belief of the kind which, I have argued, is in danger of leading to a destructive schismogenesis. Thus the search for a unified metaphysics remains either an intellectual pastime having no important effects on human action, or it leads belief into the dangerous confinement of a single dimension.

Essentially the same point has been made by one of the most profound of contemporary literary philosophers, Albert Camus.[1] His work *The Myth of Sisyphus* is an extended discussion of the impasse to which man comes when he tries to encompass the whole universe in a single unified system. 'That nostalgia

[1] Camus, A., 1955. *The Myth of Sisyphus* (Translated Justin O'Brien). Knopf, New York.

for unity,' he writes, 'that appetite for the absolute illustrates the essential impulse of the human drama.' He goes on to show what happens as the intellectual attempt to understand the world proceeds. 'At the final stage you teach me that this wondrous and multi-coloured universe can be reduced to the electron. All this is good, and I wait for you to continue. But you tell me of an invisible planetary system in which electrons gravitate around a nucleus. You explain this world to me with an image. I realize then that you have been reduced to poetry. I shall never know. . . . So that science that was to teach me everything ends up in a hypothesis. . . . A stranger to myself and to the world, armed solely with a thought that negates itself as soon as it asserts, what is this condition in which I can have peace only by refusing to know and to live?' This faces man, Camus suggests, with the necessity of deciding soberly whether suicide is not the only sensible course of action. Other philosophers, he points out, such as the existentialists Chestov, Husserl and Kierkegaard, escape from the dilemma by some variety of 'leap' into mysticism or religion—a 'leap' which is called for exactly because it cannot be rationally justified. Camus himself rejects such so-called solutions; and also suicide. His answer is a romantic one: 'I draw from the absurd three consequences, which are my revolt, my freedom and my passion . . . To a man devoid of blinders, there is no finer sight than that of an intelligence at grips with a reality that transcends it. The sight of human pride is unequalled. No disparagement is of any use.'

To the pedestrian Anglo-Saxon, and also perhaps to most empirical scientists, this furore over the impossibility of attaining a total synthetic knowledge of the universe appears a little hysterical. A key point is actually alluded to by Camus in an aside at an earlier stage in his argument. 'If I were a tree among trees, a cat among animals, this life would have a meaning, or rather this problem would not arise, because I would belong to this world.' But that, surely, is just what man is; an animal, of a peculiar kind it is true, among other animals. His knowledge of the universe, at any point in history, is the existing state of a continually developing two-way process of interaction between his evolving mental apparatus and an evolving world. In such a system, a final all-inclusive understanding is not merely unattainable, it is something which we are not called upon to yearn for. As Camus himself writes: 'I don't know whether this world has a meaning that transcends it. But I know that I do not know that meaning and that it is impossible for me just now to know it. What can a meaning outside my condition mean to me?' And it is more than that. Not only can we not seek for stability, or what Camus calls 'peace', by searching after a complete system of thought, but we should recognize that such a system, if it could be found, would bring to an end the process of evolution which is the essence of the whole world of living things of which man is a part.

These severe strictures on the elaboration of systems of thought must be counter-balanced by another consideration. Stability is not the only desideratum which we should wish to achieve in the human mind. In fact, if it were not that present-day society is suffering so grievously from mental instability and unbalance, one would probably have been tempted to place much less emphasis on the necessity for a counter-balance of beliefs than I have done in this chapter. From a more general point of view than the purely contemporary, the outstanding characteristic of the human evolutionary mechanism is the width of the field of experience and achievement which it throws open to the individual. The process of social learning offers to him a large part of the thoughts and attainments of his ancestors. A man's life, it may be said, is not restricted to his own existence, as is a dog's. It is primarily on this account that the human method of variation and selection has proved so far more rapid, and to produce such far greater effects, than the normal biological procedure. It is, therefore, obviously a prime requirement of the belief-system that it should not unduly restrict, but should rather enlarge in as great a degree as possible, the breadth and scope of the social heritage which the individual is willing to acknowledge, test and possibly accept. An ideal, to be worthy of belief, should be on a large scale.

This consideration goes some way to mitigate the apparent particularism of our previous conclusion. It may be easy enough to set up a stable personality on the basis of a belief structure comprising a primary attachment to, say, the cause of the Society for the Prevention of Cruelty to Animals, counterbalanced by a degree of devotion to the exacting, but quite different, God who rules over the game of golf. But these ideals are unduly restricted in their field of application. If mankind in general adopted them as the basis for civilization, we might perhaps be spared the dangers of a destructive schismogenesis, which leads to the committing of terrible crimes in the name of the very ideals which are supposed to prevent such conduct, but it is obvious that the richness and depth of our culture would shrink to pitiful dimensions. It is true, of course, that concentration on a restricted ideal by a given individual may enable him to devote to it sufficient energy to produce a noteworthy result; and to that extent, society may be the gainer from the impoverishment of the beliefs of some of its members. But what may be true of single persons is not necessarily applicable to society as a whole. There can be no doubt that if the generally accepted ideals of belief in a society are narrow in their scope, the richness of civilization must suffer, and the belief-structure partially fail in its function of mediating the acceptance by the individual of the cultural heritage offered him by the past.

This line of thought might at first sight lead to the conclusion that we should, after all, seek an all-embracing ideal. But not only does that seem inevitably to lead, as I have argued above, to an unstable and potentially dangerous internal conflict, but it is also at present intellectually impossible of attainment. No philosophical system yet proposed really accommodates all the values which man has formed from his experience. The acceptance of one system, as the final and comprehensive scheme to which everything may be referred, must lead to an undue restriction of the fullness of civilization even before the schismogenesis to which it will give rise becomes a practical danger. The best we can do is to see that each of the set of complementary ideals which we adopt is as all-embracing as it can be within the limits of its own field. Thus, if one accepts an attachment to a political ideal formulated in terms of a national loyalty, the larger the national organization chosen, the less likely it is to restrict the range of values which can be appreciated. Similarly, greater scope will be offered if the ideal is formulated in general terms, rather than taken to involve precisely defined and particularized characteristics. A politico-economic belief in, for instance, free trade, or communal ownership, is more limiting than a devotion to the cause of increasing the material standard of living, or enlarging the possibilities for individual development

The functions proper to the belief-structure of the mind are, potentially, best filled by ideals which are of extremely wide range. The brotherly love of the Christians, the intellectual curiosity and good sense of the Greeks, even the orderly British ideal of conduct appropriate to one's station in life, were beliefs general enough in character to apply to almost all the situations which arise in a full and active life. While representing very clearly the ultimate parental authority on which the whole process of social learning rests, they reflect this as a leading and guiding, rather than a merely restraining influence. The more particular beliefs, such as those in nationalism or free trade, which were mentioned above, can be regarded as incomplete derivatives of one or other of the more general ideals. Unfortunately, there is undoubtedly a strong tendency for such partial ideas to assume a more dynamic role within the personality than the more general ones. The broader and deeper the scope of an idea, the harder it is for the mind to grasp it in its general significance, or to apply it to particular instances. An intellectual formulation of such a belief must, indeed, be of a highly abstract nature, and is beyond the capacity of any but a highly-trained mind. Non-intellectual people may, of course, apprehend such ideals; in fact it sometimes appears as if it is easier to attain to a really profound ideal by some unformulated process of an intuitive nature than by close abstract reflection—we must all have met instances of the simple good man. But even these are all too rare. The beliefs one notices as operative in the personalities one meets are usually focused on some comparatively minor particular, some specific political or religious or ethical point. A devotion which constantly refers back to one of the great large-scale ideals of humanity is something of a rarity in human characters

197

as they are formed by society at the present day. It is surely one of the major tasks of civilization to remedy this, to see that as the child's reverence and love passes on from its parents to some wider authority, it finds itself in the presence not merely of a particular doctrine but directly confronted with the major premises of human society.

There are several current ideals of breadth and scope sufficient to rank among the mainsprings of civilization. Perhaps it is not always realized that science, as it has grown under the co-operative efforts of so many men, has by now become one of the most compelling of the possible candidates for the position of internal authority in the human belief-structure. Its adequacy to this role is often denied, chiefly by those who interpret the scientific ideal in an unduly narrow way. If Christianity meant no more than the strict adherence to the tenets of a particular fervent and narrow-minded sect (say, the Fundamentalists of Tennessee) it would seem a poor and dangerous basis on which to try to continue the culture of Western civilization. Equally, if science is thought to mean no more than an exclusive attention to the data of physics, chemistry and physiology, and to demand the dismissal of all other aspects of human experience, it also appears a threadbare and puerile belief. But the scientific attitude of mind is a much more profound embodiment of the human spirit than such a shallow view suggests.[1] I shall not attempt to formulate it in a few words; but science can approach and discuss even the subtlest problems of human conduct and of the relations between a man and his fellows.

I would not say that the scientific ideal alone is a wholly adequate foundation for the good life of the individual, or the highest civilization of society; but my main reason for this is the conviction, the grounds for which I have given earlier, that no single ideal is sufficient. The authority of science gives its sanction to one of the greatest creations of the human mind— the attitude of logical thought continually checked by the empirical appeal to experiment—but it needs, in my view, to be supplemented by the ideal of the creative artist—an ideal which expresses itself in thought-processes which move in a different

[1] Cf. my *The Scientific Attitude*.

dimension to those of logic and experiment.

These two ideals—the combination of reason and empiricism which is usually held to comprise the whole of science, and the creative imagination or intuition which is considered to be characteristic of art—form a dualism in different dimensions, of the kind I have been discussing. Actually a simultaneous belief in both of them is already incorporated in the practice, though not usually explicitly in the theory, of scientific work. Logic and experiment begin only after intuition has apprehended the problem. A really new scientific idea, of wave-mechanics, or genes, or even a new hunch about some quite specialized and technical matter, is an imaginative production, dependent on faculties which do not differ in kind from those which gave rise to Cubism or *Ulysses*.

Neither of this pair of partners is sufficient in itself. The combination of empirical experiment with logical thought, although a powerful tool, would soon run out of materials to work on if it was quite divorced from intuitive insight. The inadequacy of 'the creative process' alone, unchecked by logic and empirical observation, has I think been rather conclusively demonstrated in recent years by the failure of those schools of art which have laid an almost exclusive emphasis on it—schools such as Dada, Surrealism and, dare one say, even in most instances the fashionable 'abstract expressionism'—to produce anything which looks in the slightest durable. Effective creation, indeed, demands the co-operation of an intuitive faculty—of that non-logical activity which is often undeservedly referred to as 'the creative process' *tout court*, or by more cautious psychologists[1] as 'the preconscious process'—but it also requires some contribution, whose importance varies with the context but can never be negligible, of the logical and empirical faculties.

This dualism, of all the possible choices open to a child growing up in our time, is the most effective in carrying out the functions of the belief-structure of the human mind, namely, of enabling man to use the experience of past generations as an aid in coming to grips with the world as he finds it. In the words of Yeats:

[1] E.g. Kubie.

Civilization is hooped together, brought
Under a rule, under the semblance of peace
By manifold illusion: but man's life is thought,
And he, despite his terror, cannot cease
Ravening through century after century,
Ravening, raging, and uprooting that he may come
Into the desolation of reality.

If we cannot hope to abolish the beliefs or 'illusions' on which human social life is based, at least we should choose such as are large enough to accommodate the major part of reality, and are of a kind which facilitate man's gradual approach to it: and, while acknowledging the force of the poet's sense of the essential tragedy of life, be somewhat unwilling to dismiss the whole of reality as a desolation.

CHAPTER 16

Biological Wisdom and the Problems of Today

THE discussions in the last few chapters do not, in my opinion, provide any reason for rejecting the broad outline of the argument which is summarized in Chapter 2. Indeed, their main result has been to strengthen several points which at that time were less firmly anchored.

In particular, our deeper understanding, both of the results of evolution, and of the processes by which it has been brought about, provide considerable reinforcement for the argument that ethical beliefs play an essential role in enabling the human race to continue evolving in a direction which in general terms continues that of animal anagenesis, but by a mechanism which is peculiarly characteristic of *homo sapiens*. We have reason for believing that although some evolutionary lines may persist with little change for long periods, while others may actually retrogress or exhibit a mere increase in diversity, there are bound to be some sequences of forms in which the pressure of natural selection leads to an actual improvement—which we know technically as an anagenesis—in some or all aspects of the evolutionary system. We can see that among such improvements at some time or other there is every likelihood to expect an increase in the effectiveness with which information is transmitted from one generation to the next. The specific human mechanism of passing on information by social teaching and learning falls into place as an improvement of this kind. Possibly other improvements might have been conceived of, but this is the one which has actually happened.

We can see that an essential part of this mechanism is that the human being must be brought into a condition in which it will act as a receiver of the messages transmitted. Such reception involves the acceptance of authority. Ethical beliefs, which are essentially beliefs about the nature of the most authoritative demands, are a part of the human system for receiving transmitted information. This reinforces our original conclusion that the function of ethical beliefs is to make possible human evolution according to the mode which it is following. We can, therefore, justifiably proceed, as we did earlier, to conclude that an examination of the direction of evolution—in particular, its anagenesis—can provide us with a criterion from which we can judge whether any particular ethical system is fulfilling this function efficiently or not.

It is important to notice how much is being claimed in this argument. This can perhaps best be realized by contrast with a less far-reaching formulation. In his *Touchstone for Ethics* Julian Huxley wrote (p. 32):

'Furthermore, since in the process of evolution values emerge, they must be taken into account by the scientist. We find values not merely emerging from the evolutionary process, but playing an active part in its latest phase; we know as an immediate and obvious fact that there are higher and lower values; we discover as a result of scientific analysis that there are more and less desirable or valuable directions in evolution. And so it comes about that, since the extended scientific world-view based on the theory of evolution must take account of mind and values, it is capable of performing a function which a purely physical world-view can never achieve: in addition to providing us with knowledge and an intellectual outlook and approach, it can give us guidance. It can thus aid in the construction of a scientific morality. . . .'

I am arguing that the connection between ethical values and human evolution is very much closer than this quotation suggests. It is not merely the case that values have in fact emerged; what I am claiming is that the specifically human mode of evolution, based on socio-genetic transmission of information, essentially requires the existence, as a functional part of the mechanism, of something which must have many of the characteristics of ethical belief. It is necessary, before socio-genetic transmission can operate, that some sort of 'authority-bearing system' is formed in the mental apparatus of those who will transmit and those who will receive.

It is only if this phase of the argument is accepted that we can escape from Huxley's uncomfortable reliance on the supposition that 'we know as an immediate and obvious fact that there are higher and lower values'. We may, perhaps, 'know' this, in the sense that introspection discloses such a conviction in us, but surely we cannot be said to 'know' it in the sense that we can hope to persuade a sceptic of it. If, however, the arguments given above are valid, we can arrive at a criterion for attempting to assess the degree to which the various systems of higher and lower values which various people 'know' are biologically 'wise'.

Even if something resembling ethical belief is a necessary part of socio-genetic transmission, that does not of course imply that the existing human system is the only possible, or even the most efficient, type of mechanism conceivable. From the point of view of evolution, all that is required is that human beings should be able to act as receivers of transmitted information. The actual authoritative system set up in human minds seems commonly to carry much more weight than would be necessary to fulfil this function adequately enough. Certainly as yet we understand this situation very little, and are hardly in a position to say just how strong our ethical beliefs, or in psychoanalytical terms, our super-ego, ought to be for maximum efficiency; but the prevalence of individual neurotic disorder connected with super-ego formation and function, and, in particular, the horrifying effects of social actions based on excessive beliefs of an allegedly ethical character, as they are exhibited in the wars and persecutions in the name of religion, politics, nationalism, racism and various other idealisms, is sufficient evidence that the human condition might well be improved. Psychoanalysis and general biology agree with the age-old intuition of mankind in concluding that the step from the animal condition—evolution based on the biological genetic system—to the human—evolution based on a socio-genetic mechanism—has involved something which may not unjustifiably be termed original sin. In Freud's words, quoted before, it is an uneven and careless piece of work.

The viewpoint which sees these phenomena in the light of their bearing on general evolution again provides us with a criterion from which they can be judged. One can use the direction of evolution to assess, not only the nature of the ethical ideals believed in, but to evaluate the character of the belief itself. It is too simple to consider belief an all-or-nothing affair, that you either believe or do not believe. In the intellectual sphere scientists have long accustomed themselves to the impossibility of complete belief in anything. Some knowledge is accepted, and accepted firmly enough to commit one's whole life, but the acceptance is still to some extent provisional, in that one is always prepared for further knowledge to reveal inadequacies in it. The intensity of belief which usually seems to be thought appropriate in the ethical sphere is perhaps almost always excessive. The arguments that Julian Huxley and Karin Stephen put forward (pp. 173, 174) for considering the attainment of mental health as one of the essential criteria to be used in judging ethical systems is another way of expressing this same point. The general anagenesis of evolution is towards what may crudely be called richness of experience. In the human evolutionary system, progress in this direction demands the formation of mental systems having some degree of authority, but if they have too strong an authority this tends to produce a counterbalancing opposing effect of impoverishment. The question is, can we shift the balance in such a way that the overall rate of advance is improved?

It is clearly no part of the purpose of this book to attempt to work out, even in broad outline, the nature of the conclusions to which the application of the evolutionary criteria would lead; that is, as Huxley remarked, a task for a whole generation of men as thinkers and doers, and anything more than a very summary treatment of it in this place would only create a false perspective. In general terms, our argument leads to the conclusion that biological wisdom consists in the encouragement of the forward progress (anagenesis) both of the mechanism of the socio-genetic evolutionary system, and of the changes in the grade of human organization which that system brings about. It is worthwhile to mention very briefly, without attempting to solve them, the type of problems which at the present time present the greatest challenges to such an approach.

Most ethical philosophers, when called upon to give an example of the type of problem with which their theory should deal, tend to cite some question which might arise in connection with their own behaviour—often indeed a question which could only be of much concern to middle-class individuals living in a western European culture. For instance, Broad, in the discussion of my original thesis at the Aristotelian Society, cited the dilemma of the man who had to choose between providing an adequate education for his daughter or a retirement pension for an old family retainer. No one, I suppose, would deny that the problem might be a difficult one; but I feel that one might legitimately doubt whether it is a matter of sufficient importance to serve as a typical example of the questions with which ethical theory is faced in the world of today. We can easily see around us too many examples of lives being completely ruined, or even terminated prematurely, to feel that Broad's problem is other than a rather peripheral one.

The major ethical problems of today in the context of individual-to-individual behaviour would, I think, according to our criteria, have to be sought in those types of attitude and activity which facilitate or hinder the development of a healthy authority structure. A very important aspect of this, of course, is our treatment of the developing child, but the authority structures within the mind probably go on developing and being modified even in much later stages of life. It seems probable that to a considerable extent their healthy development is conditioned by the extent to which one is treated by the other people with whom one comes in contact as a person—an individual—rather than as a representative of some abstract conception such as a racial or class group. It is at any rate those areas, whichever they may be, in which questions of general mental health are involved, that our criteria would suggest as posing the most important questions of inter-personal ethics. They are, of course, aspects of the anagenesis of the human evolutionary system.

But this system does not consist only of the authority systems of the mind. The notions about biological wisdom to which we have come suggest that great importance should be attached to considerations concerning the general conditions of human communication; and in fact many problems are at present arising in this field, which we are beginning to realize are, or should be accepted as, essentially ethical problems. These are the problems of national independence and international organization.

The fact of social communication produces an organization of the evolving human population which is radically different from that of most other biological systems with which one might at first be tempted to compare it. In so far as there are subordinate groupings within the human species, they can influence one another in much more varied and much more thorough ways than the parts of other biological systems can. In the sub-human world, locally differentiated populations either remain independent, except for a restricted amount of gene-flow mediated by migration and intercrossing; or one supplants and eliminates the other. In man, an enormously greater proportion of the socially transmissible heritage of China is immediately available to Peru, and vice versa. Again, in an animal body the different tissues have a profound influence on one another's development only at certain restricted times, and then in the main by facilitating one or other of a few alternatives, as in embryonic induction and the like; there is here nothing comparable to the long continued and subtly differentiated interactions between, say, Britain and France, or China and Japan. The problems of the organization of the human species are *sui generis*; very little help concerning them can be found by looking either at evolving animal species or developing animal individuals.

Failure to realize this has notoriously led to the propounding of many fallacious and deceptive parallels between social affairs and biological systems. The attempt to consider human evolution in animal terms led to the aberrations of Social Darwinism. Comparisons between human society and animal organisms are no more satisfactory. There is a whole train of literature devoted to such a theme, from Hobbes' *Leviathan* to such recent productions as Morley Roberts' *The Behaviour of Nations*, which roundly classes nations 'without any metaphor or figure of speech' as low-grade invertebrates.

Very few responsible biologists would admit to taking such analogies seriously, but even some of the best of them have been tempted to toy with similar notions. For instance, Julian Huxley in his introduction to Teilhard de Chardin's *The Phenomenon of Man* writes: 'His formulation, however, is more profound and more seminal: it implies we should consider inter-humanity as a new type of organism, whose destiny it is to realize new possibilities for evolving life on this planet. Accordingly, we should endeavour to equip it with the mechanisms necessary for the proper fulfilment of its task—the psycho-social equivalents of sense-organs, effector-organs, and a co-ordinating central nervous system with dominant brain; and our aim should be the gradual personalization of the human unit of evolution—its conversion, on the new level of co-operative thinking, into the equivalent of a person.'

This seems to me to pre-judge a great many very ticklish problems. In an animal body the muscles cannot communicate directly with the secreting cells of the hormonal glands or the absorbing cells of the gut. Co-ordination of function has in these circumstances been achieved by the evolution of a nervous system, finally by a dominating brain. In the world community of man, all the geographically separate parts can be, and in fact are, in close communication with one another. The animal parallel is false. It is quite illegitimate to draw from it the conclusion that human society requires a dominant co-ordinating centre, which is separated geographically or in any other way from the rest of the body of mankind.

The type of organization which would seem most appropriate to a complex made up inter-communicating parts must be something quite different from the organization appropriate to an entity whose parts cannot directly influence one another. It would seem reasonable to suppose, for instance, that rigid separation of function, such as we find when we compare the muscles, the skeleton, the intestine, and so on of an animal, in mankind is unattainable, even if desirable. On the other hand, it clearly does not follow that we should aim at rushing to the other extreme, by attempting to reduce the whole of the human species to complete uniformity. In practice, of course, at the present time, although there is perhaps some tendency towards reducing the differences between the local varieties of human culture, we still find a rich diversity in the ways in which different groups of men choose to conduct their lives. Indeed, at the present period in history two conflicting tendencies are clearly at work: one, the spread over the entire world of the methods and outlook of the science which grew up first in western Europe; and secondly, the insistence on the value and vitality of local differentiations. These differentiations are sometimes claimed to be based on the concept of race, sometimes on that of nations; and feelings which are expressed in terms of these two concepts are some of the most powerful in human affairs today.

Both notions have very considerable justification in natural facts; both have valuable contributions to make to the organization of the human species as an evolving entity. However, they are both somewhat imprecise, and can easily be carried to lengths at which they become dangerous. Throughout his history man seems never to have been a very stationary type of organism, with sub-division of the human species in the geographically separated populations which would be necessary for the evolution of clearly distinguishable races. At least on the small scale the situation has been extensively confused by migrations and the intermingling of slightly divergent groups. It is probably reasonable enough to recognize racial distinctions between the 'whites' (Europeans, North Americans, Australians, etc.), the African peoples, the Asian peoples, and so on. Those who have for so long been profoundly aware of being the 'White-Man' should now be ready to recognize and welcome the formation of an African consciousness and an Asian consciousness, which is inevitable as communication between the various parts of those regions of the globe become more highly developed. It is when one tries to apply the concept of race to smaller regions than the continents, or the major parts of them, that the notion begins to evaporate under one's hand. Even such relatively large and isolated portions of the earth's surface as India and China cannot easily be regarded as having given rise to a distinguishable Indian or Chinese race; biologically speaking, their populations consist of very many races and of innumerable hybrids between them. Such unity as they have—which may be very real—cannot be founded solely on biological characteristics, but depends on an important admixture of nationalist feelings which arise from their political history. There is indeed a very rough inverse relation between the area inhabited by a distinctive and unified population and the importance of biological race in determining this unity. Even in the largest areas, such as Asia, Africa or western Europe, the political feelings—i.e. 'nationalist' feelings in the widest use of that term—play a not unimportant role in creating a feeling of unity. When we come to relatively small areas, such as Scotland, Switzerland, Ghana or Ceylon, feelings of unity within their populations must arise entirely from causes other than their biological characteristics.

If we regard the human species as something which is involved in a process of evolution carried out by means of social communication, it would seem to follow that the optimum organization would be one in which there were, in the first place, locally differentiated communities which would have something to communicate to one another, and, in the second, means of full communication between them. The development of differentiated local groupings of the human populations would therefore seem to be advantageous. It is, of course, a question how large these groupings should be. If each group was large enough to be definable mainly in racial terms there could be only very few of them. On the other hand, there has clearly been a tendency in the last few hundred years for some of the smaller groupings which originally considered themselves distinct to lose their identity in larger units. For instance, in England the distinction between Yorkshiremen and Cockneys is much less definite than it was a hundred years ago; Burgundians and Gascons are rapidly becoming just Frenchmen; and Yorubas are developing into Nigerians and perhaps into West Africans. Somewhere in this range between the local tribe and the continental race there is presumably a more or less optimum size of grouping. I doubt if we know yet just where it is.

The most advantageous degree of local differentiation within human populations will in fact almost certainly depend on the extent to which man successfully organizes communication between the groups. Here again it is some intermediate between two conceivable extremes which would seem likely to be best. Very inadequate communication, such as has existed throughout most of past history, has the effect of denying to some local groups the advantages which men in other parts of the globe have already achieved; as, for instance, the inhabitants of much of the earth's surface were denied the advantage of modern science until adequate channels of communication were opened up. On the other hand, it might lead to an impoverishment if communication were so complete that the various regions of the earth could not work out, with some independence, the characteristic cultures based on their own particular insights. It has, surely, been to the advantage of man as a whole that western Europe has explored in depth the riches inherent in Christian, Greek and Roman tradition, that China has developed a massive civilization based on Confucius and Buddha, and the other major regions followed their own genius. Greater communication between the various systems of culture is now very desirable, but it would surely only be a matter for regret if communications in the past had been, or in the future become, so perfect as to confuse a development of individual character.

From this point of view one must, I think, welcome in the name of biological wisdom the dawning—if it does dawn—of a period of 'co-existence' between the two major cultural forces of the world today, those deriving from what we may loosely call Capitalism on the one side, and Communism on the other. Both these systems are rapidly evolving, as all human affairs must do, and it would be quite inappropriate here to attempt to describe either of them as they stand at present. But any impartial consideration of them must surely suggest that both contain much of value and also much which is to be deplored. The complete obliteration of either would gravely impoverish what one might call the 'Idea Pool' of the human species: the store of socially-transmittable variations which are available as the raw material for future evolution. When one is dealing with a relatively localized cultural development with a narrow range of ideas, such as Nazism was, the elimination of the whole thing may be advantageous if that rids man of a number of ideas which impede anagenesis, at the expense of only a few potentially valuable ones. Both Capitalism and Communism are too large-scale, both in their geographical extent and in the range and importance of the aspects of human life which they affect, for such elimination to be wise, even if it were possible. The state of co-existence towards which we are rather reluctantly being driven is, in my opinion, the condition to which biological wisdom would lead us.

The advantages of such co-existence will only be fully developed if there is considerable communication between the two groups. Throughout past history right up to the present day, one of the most important methods for social transmission between human groups has been warfare. Religions and other forms of social organization have been carried into new countries by Christian Crusaders or by Mohammed's horsemen, just as Communism in our day has been carried in a similar way into much of eastern Europe. But mankind is now faced by a new situation. The development of industrial societies based on scientific technology has led on the one hand to the polarization of the human race into only a few huge power complexes, and on the other to the production of physical and biological weapons capable of causing death and the destruction of human artefacts on an altogether unprecedented scale.

These two factors have clearly entirely transformed the nature of warfare. A conflict between the major human groups in which the newer methods were used would, it seems, be certain to bring about the destruction of by far the greater part, if not the whole, of the human race, and the destruction of almost all the material structures by which man had modified his environment. Any attempt by one group to impose its socially transmissible heritage on the other by means of warfare would involve paying a price of this order of magnitude. Moreover, the price that even the winning group—if there was one—would have to pay would be so enormous that it is inconceivable that its ideas at the end of the process would be the same as they had been at the beginning. What, if anything, it could impose on its defeated enemy would certainly not be that which it had originally intended to impose. Even in the last two world wars, the strains involved in the activity of warfare itself were so great that victors almost equally with vanquished came out of it quite different from what they had been at the beginning. In any atomic and biological war the metamorphosis of the contestants would certainly be even more complete. One may be rather confident that warfare as it exists today can no longer be used as a means of spreading a social system from one major human grouping to another.

The problem of modern war is to be considered not only as an aspect of the mechanism of human evolution; it is the context in which we face most sharply at the present time the problems of the continued anagenesis which that mechanism should bring about. The cost of an all-out war to the human species would seem to be the loss of at least a very large fraction of man's store of artefacts. The enrichment of the human condition which our evolution has brought about since the Neolithic period depends very greatly on the structures and mechanisms which man has fabricated. The loss of these would be a reversal of anagenesis on an enormous scale; something perhaps comparable to the wiping out of the whole vertebrate stock at the end of the Mesozoic. I find it very difficult to believe that it would be worth paying this material price either to ensure or to prevent the domination of any one of the ideologies or cultural systems—which are after all very flexible and impermanent things on an evolutionary time-scale—which have been developed by any of the major power blocks at this relatively advanced stage of human history.

To the material cost we should have to add that in human life. There is a very real danger that an all-out war would bring the whole human race to an end, subjecting our species to the extinction which has overtaken so many other animal species in the geological past. Even to run a serious risk of such an event must certainly be considered the nadir of biological wisdom. One sometimes hears the argument advanced that if even only a few million human beings survived, the damage of a major war could eventually be overcome. That may well be so; but the time that would be required before the lost ground was made good would surely be very long in comparison with the period that would, without war, suffice for the normal processes of evolution to change out of all recognition the ideologies and cultures of the world as we know them today.

I can see no escape from the conclusion that the major ethical task for today is to ensure that a major war does not occur. It would be inappropriate here to attempt any discussion of the ways in which this aim is most likely to be achieved. It by no means follows, from the remarks about the destructiveness of warfare made above, that the most sensible policy for any of the major powers would be an immediate abolition of all its armed forces.

Consideration of the ethical status of war confronts us with the extremely complex and difficult problem of the attitude that should be adopted towards death and killing. In an evolutionary process carried out by the biological methods of genetics, the death of individuals is a necessary part of the whole system. In theory this need not be the case in an evolutionary system which operates through the social transmission of information. We seem, however, still to be a very long way from abolishing man's biological limitations which lead him into senescence and death. It is scarcely realistic to discuss human evolution except in terms that concede that it will in the foreseeable future be founded on biological evolution, so that the death of individuals will be a necessary part of it. We have perhaps in recent times been moving too rapidly towards a standpoint from which death is considered inherently a bad thing in itself. We have instead to accept the fact that, in spite of the advances which man has made in some respects over his biological predecessors, it still remains an essential part of his nature.

To bring about the death of another human individual has always been considered by all men a very important action, but the degree to which it is considered an ethically bad action varies considerably in different communities. Societies such as those founded on head-hunting, or on warfare, or even those which merely condone duelling, have taken a relatively permissive attitude towards it. We cannot therefore claim as some authors have done that the prohibition 'Thou shalt not kill' is an inherent and unalterable ethical human value. However one can easily see good biological reasons why killing is rather generally, even if not universally and in all circumstances, held to be evil. At a relatively crude level of argument, it is clear that the killing of one member of a human group by another member of the same group will tend for a number of reasons to lead to the weakening of that social unit. During much of human history there must have been a powerful intergroup natural selection, and this would lead to the spread of hereditary factors which would tend to inhibit behaviour of such an anti-social kind. This is the process of the biological evolution of altruism as Haldane and Muller have discussed it; the process which Chauncey Leake christened 'ethicogenesis'. In my opinion it is likely to have had some, but only a restricted, importance.

The more important determinants of man's ethical attitude towards killing are to be found in the social rather than in the biological sphere. There is, in the first place, the fact that our ethical beliefs originate in experiences with our parents and others which initially inculcate lessons of co-operation and sympathy with other individuals. However much this substratum may become overlaid in the later developments of the super-ego, every man's ethical beliefs are bound to begin with a bias in this direction. Again, at quite a different level, we must recognize that the anagenesis of man has been towards the production of personalities capable of an ever richer experience, which arises in the main from his interactions with other people in his social environment; and the type of inter-personal experience of which a man is capable is not independent of the permissiveness of his ethical system towards killing. Men who can with equanimity bring about the death of another human being are in general characterized by some insensitivity towards other individuals, and this insensitivity is likely to be increased if an act of killing is actually performed. It is, I think, these considerations concerning the killer, rather than those concerning the person killed, which have played the major part in bringing about the evolution of the widespread condemnation in modern societies of practices such as duelling, or the murderous violence of the Italian Renaissance, or even capital punishment. And it is on grounds such as these that, if we look at human ethical systems from the standpoint of evolution, we can conclude that, although death is a biological necessity, an ethical system which condemns the procurement of the death of a human individual is to be commended.

This discussion of the ethics of death may seem to have laboured a well-worn theme and to have reached a trite conclusion. The reason why it seemed necessary to consider the topic at some length is that we are at present faced by rather novel questions about the ethical value of the mere fact of life or of death. On the one hand, there is now, as was pointed out in the introduction, a practical possibility of doubling the expected span of life of all those who are born in that vast region of the world which is only just receiving the benefits of modern science. How great an ethical value should be attached to postponing their deaths? On the other hand, the same scientific advances have the consequence that, if man reproduces as fast as his present sexual instincts tempt him to do, the numbers of the human population will in a few generations outrun the practical possibilities of providing them all with a full and rich life.[1] We seem to be faced with the unavoidable necessity of denying man's gonadotropic hormones some of their natural outcome in new births. How much ethical condemnation should be attached to this 'denial of life' to certain unutilized gametes?

The arguments about the ethics of death given above suggest that the answer to these problems is to be looked for in a consideration of the richness of experience of those people who actually become members of the human community, rather than in any immediate attention to the facts of life or death as such. The denial of life to the unborn by the practice of contraception in one of its many forms cannot be condemned as doing harm to *them*. It is from this point of view no more ethically bad than the enormously greater wastage of gametes which is a normal part of the biological existence of most animals, including man. In so far as it has ethical consequences, these are to be looked for in the effect the various practices may have on the character of the husband and wife who carry them out—a matter in which it is

[1] It has been calculated that if the whole population of the earth had since the time of the Pharaohs increased in numbers as fast as the population of Egypt has been doing in the last few decades, the living mass of the human species would by now be the size of an astronomical nebula and the circumference of the mass would be receding from its centre with the speed of light.

not very difficult to find reasonably satisfactory solutions—or on the genetical structure of the social group as a whole—a matter for eugenics. From the same point of view, we should form our ethical estimation of measures to increase the average life-span of the peoples of the under-developed countries in terms of the effect which those measures may have on the richness of their experience. The conclusion must surely follow that the application of modern scientific and technological methods to improving the human situation in the backward countries is the greatest ethical good which mankind has within its grasp at this period of history. It would amount to the spreading over the whole of the human race of the evolutionary advances which so far have been made by only a small part of it.

That part of the species which has already made these advances —that is to say, western Europe and North America, who are so rapidly being joined by Russia and a few other countries—can give very considerable assistance to the other countries which are struggling to catch up with them. But there are limits to this. Too much and too thorough 'assistance' would bring the danger of swamping the individuality of the recipient groups, and thus reducing the world to too great a homogeneity. In practice, most of the previously under-developed countries exhibit strong and, one is inclined to admit, very reasonable desires to work out their own salvation, with only rather restricted assistance from outside. This means that the more advanced nations cannot devote anything like their whole forces directly to the achievement of the major positive human good of the present day—although certainly they could devote much more than they are doing at present.

They should be looking for other tasks of ethical value, more appropriate to their actual position. It would not be difficult to find them. Perhaps the most important would be one which might be christened the 'conquest of the conquest of nature'. Existing or immediately foreseeable scientific and technical advances have relieved mankind in the advanced countries of most infectious diseases, provided him with almost complete protection from any damaging effects of the external environment, and are rapidly taking off his shoulders nearly the whole burden of physical work which has weighed him down since Adam delved and Eve span. To a limited but fairly satisfactory extent we can say that man has conquered non-human nature. But it is surely clear that we have not yet discovered the best way of using that conquest. Our buildings and machines have been thrown together with the primary object of relieving us of our physical burdens. It is a commonplace that they subject us to mental and psychological strains which are quite difficult to bear. Our vast conurbations, with their nerve-shattering traffic systems, may save us from many of the physical miseries of our ancestors, but it is impossible to believe that they provide the optimum environment in which to live a good life. Over the horizon of the near future we can see the prospect of vastly increased leisure, as atomic energy, machine tools and automation take over most of the drudgery of fabrication. Again it is a platitude to say that we shall not know what to do with this leisure when we get it.

Here surely are a series of problems in which a new step in human evolutionary advance is called for. From the point of view I have been putting forward, here is area in which some of the greatest ethical values are to be sought. To work out the type or types of physical environment which modern techniques could create for man, and to discover new and richer ways of conducting one's life within them, are tasks which call for the most devoted service from those who wish to devote their endeavours to furthering the good. There is still far too little effort expended in this direction. A few architects follow the lead of Corbusier and Gropius in considering the man-made environment as a place to live in, a few Utopians and writers such as Lewis Mumford or Hannah Arendt discuss the human condition and how it might be improved, but such endeavours are scattered and individual.

From the point of view of an evolutionary ethics it would be reasonable if the advanced countries were devoting themselves to this problem as whole-heartedly and as vigorously as the under-developed countries are striving to overcome their physical difficulties. To conceive of, and to bring into being, the human environment and ways of living which make full use of our conquest of nature is a task for both scientists and humanists together. The latter too often fear that the scientists would introduce only a hard, inhuman technical civilization. Perhaps I can finish this discussion by reminding them that the last first-class scientist who gave a concrete expression of the kind of life he felt mankind might lead was Piero Della Francesca.

REFERENCES

ANSCOMBE, G. E. M., "Modern Moral Philosophy," *Philosophy*, **33** (1958), p. 1.

ARENDT, H., *The Human Condition*, Chicago, Chicago University Press, 1959.

AYER, A. J., *Language, Truth and Logic*, New York, Dover Publications, Inc., 1951.

AYER, A. J., *The Problem of Knowledge*, New York, St. Martin's Press, Inc., 1957.

BALINT, M., *Thrills and Regressions*, New York, International Universities Press, Inc., 1959.

BATESON, G., "Social Planning and the Concept of Deutero-learning," Conference on Science, Philosophy and Religion, New York, Harper & Brothers, 1942, p. 81.

BATESON, G., *Naven*, Palo Alto, California, Stanford University Press, 1958.

BATESON, G., "The New Conceptual Frames for Behavioral Research," 6th Annual Psychiat. Institute Conference, 1959.

BATESON, G., "Minimal Requirements for a Theory of Schizophrenia," Albert D. Lasker Memorial Lecture, Chicago, 1959.

BEACH, F. A., and JAYNES, J., "Effects of Early Experience upon the Behavior of Animals," *Psychol. Bull.*, **51** (1954), p. 239.

BROAD, C. D., *Five Types of Ethical Theory*, New York, Harcourt, Brace & Co., 1930.

BROAD, C. D., "Symposium on the Relation Between Science and Ethics," *Proc. Aristotelian Soc.*, p. 101.

BYNNER, W., *The Way of Life According to Laotzu*, New York, John Day & Co., 1944.

CARNAP, R., *Philosophy and Logical Syntax*, London, Kegan Paul, 1935.

DE CHARDIN, P. TEILHARD, *The Phenomenon of Man*, New York, Harper & Bros., 1959.

CHILDE, V. G., *What Happened in History*, Baltimore, Penguin Books, Inc., 1946.

CONKLIN, E. G., *Man: Real and Ideal*, New York, Chas. Scribner's Sons, 1943.

CRITCHLEY, M., "The Evolution of Man's Capacity for Language," *Evolution after Darwin*, 2 (1959), 289, Chicago, University of Chicago Press.

DARLING, F. F., *A Herd of Red Deer*, New York, Oxford University Press, 1937.

DARLINGTON, C. D., *The Evolution of Genetic Systems*, New York, Macmillan Co., 1939.

DARLINGTON, C. D., *The Facts of Life*, New York, Macmillan Co., 1955.

DOBZHANSKY, T., *The Biological Basis of Human Freedom*, New York, Columbia University Press, 1956.

ELIOT, T. S., *Notes Towards the Definition of Culture*, New York, Harcourt, Brace and Co., 1949.

EMERSON, A. E., "The Evolution of Behavior Among Social Insects," *Evolution and Behavior*, A. Roe and G. G. Simpson, New Haven, Yale University Press, 1958.

EMMET, D. M., "The Choice of a World Outlook," *Philosophy*, 23 (1948), p. 217.

EWING, A. C., *The Definition of Good*, New York, Macmillan Co., 1947.

FISHER, E. M., "Habits of the Southern Sea-Otter," *Journal of Mammalogy*, 20 (1939), p. 21.

FREUD, A., *The Ego and the Mechanisms of Defence*, New York, International Universities Press, 1946.

FREUD, S., *Totem and Taboo*, New York, Macmillan Co., 1953.

FRISCH, K. V., *Bees: Their Vision, Chemical Senses and Language*, Ithaca, Cornell University Press, 1950.

GELLNER, E. A., "Reflections on Linguistic Philosophy," *The Listener*, August, 1957.

GELLNER, E. A., *Words and Things*, Boston, Beacon Press, 1960.

HALDANE, J. B. S., *The Causes of Evolution*, New York, Harper & Bros., 1932.

HALLOWELL, A. I., "Self, Society and Culture in Phylogenetic Perspective," *Evolution after Darwin,* **2** (1960), Chicago, University of Chicago Press, p. 309.

HARDIE, W. F. R., "My Own Free-Will," *Philosophy,* **32** (1957), p. 21.

HARLOW, H. F., "The Formation of Learning Sets," *Psychol. Review,* **56** (1949), p. 51.

HARLOW, H. F., "Primate Learning," in *Comparative Psychology,* New York, Prentice-Hall, 1952.

HARLOW, H. F., "The Evolution of Learning," in *Evolution and Behavior,* ed. A. Roe and G. G. Simpson, New Haven, Yale University Press, 1958.

HARLOW, H. F., "Love in Infant Monkeys," *Scientific American,* June, 1959.

HEBB, B. O., and THOMPSON, W. H., "The Social Significance of Animal Studies," *Handbook of Social Psychology,* ed. G. Lindzey, Vol. 1, Reading, Mass., Wesley Publishing Co., 1954.

HEISENBERG, W., *The Physicist's Conception of Nature,* New York, Harcourt, Brace and Co., 1958.

HESS, E. H., "Imprinting in Animals," *Scientific American,* March, 1958.

HILGARD, E. R., *Theories of Learning,* New York, Appleton-Century-Crofts, Inc., 1956.

HINDE, R. A., "The Establishment of the Parent-Offspring Relationship in Birds, with some Mammalian Analogies," *Animal Behavior,* New York, Cambridge University Press, 1960.

HOFSTADTER, R., *Social Darwinism in American Thought* (revised ed.), Boston, Beacon Press, 1955.

HOLMES, S. J., *Life and Morals,* New York, Macmillan, 1948.

HUXLEY, J. S., *Man Stands Alone,* New York, Harper and Bros., 1941.

HUXLEY, J. S., *Evolution: The Modern Synthesis,* New York, Harper and Bros., 1942.

HUXLEY, J. S., *Touchstone for Ethics,* New York, Harper and Bros., 1947.

HUXLEY, J. S., "Evolution, Cultural and Biological," *Year-book of Anthropology*, ed. W. Thomas, New York, Wenner-Gren Foundation for Anthropological Research, Inc., 1955.

HUXLEY, J. S., "Evolutionary Processes and Taxonomy, with Special Reference to Grades," *Uppsala Univ. Arsskrift*, **6** (1958), p. 21.

KAPLAN, A., "Freud and Modern Philosophy," in *Freud and the Twentieth Century*, ed. B. Nelson, Gloucester, Mass., Peter Smith Co., 1958.

KLEIN, M., in *Science and Ethics*, London, Allen and Unwin, 1942, p. 83.

KLUCKHÖHN, CLYDE, "The Scientific Study of Values," in *Three Lectures*, Toronto, University of Toronto Press, 1958.

KÖHLER, O., "The Ability of Birds to 'Count,' " *Bulletin of Animal Behavior*, **9** (1950), p. 41.

KÖHLER, W., *The Mentality of Apes*, New York, Universal Distributors Co., 1948.

KROEBER, A. L., "Evolution, History and Cultures," *Evolution after Darwin*, **2** (1960), Chicago, University of Chicago Press.

KUBIE, L. S., *Neurotic Distortion of the Creative Process*, Kansas City, Kan., University of Kansas Press, 1958.

LACK, D. L., *The Life of the Robin*, London, Witherby Press, 1943.

LANGER, S., *Philosophy in a New Key*, Cambridge, Mass., Harvard University Press, 1942.

LEAKE, C. D., "Ethicogenesis," *Scientific Monthly*, **60** (1945), 245.

LEAKE, C. D., and ROMANELL, P., *Can We Agree? A Scientist and a Philosopher Argue About Ethics*, Austin, Texas, University of Texas Press, 1950.

LERNER, I. M., *Genetic Homeostasis*, New York, John Wiley & Sons, 1954.

LORENZ, K. Z., *King Solomon's Ring*, New York, Thomas Crowell Co., 1952.

LOVEJOY, A. O., *The Great Chain of Being*, New York, William Morrow, Inc., 1956.

MATHER, K., *The Listener*, October, 1959.

MEAD, M., *New Lives for Old*, New York, William Morrow, 1956.

MEAD, M., "Cultural Determinants of Behavior," *Evolution and Behavior*, A. Roe and G. G. Simpson, New Haven, Yale University Press, 1958.

MEAD, M., *An Anthropologist at Work*, New York, Houghton Mifflin Co., 1959.

MEAD, M., Terry Lectures, New Haven, 1960.

MOORE, G. E., *Principia Ethica*, New York, Cambridge University Press, 1948.

MOWRER, O. H., "The Psychologist Looks at Language," *American Psychology*, **9** (1954), p. 660.

MULLER, H. J., "Human Values in Relation to Evolution," *Science*, **127** (1958), p. 625.

MULLER, H. J., "A Hundred Years Without Darwin Are Enough," *School Science and Mathematics*, April, 1959.

NEEDHAM, J., *History is on Our Side*, New York, Macmillan Co., 1947.

NOWELL-SMITH, P. H., Ethics, London, Penguin Books, Ltd., 1954.

OAKLEY, D., "A Definition of Man," *Penguin Scientific News*, **20** (1951).

PIAGET, J., *The Moral Judgment of the Child*, New York, Harcourt, Brace & Co., 1932.

PONTECORVO, G., *Trends in Genetic Analysis*, New York, Columbia University Press, 1959.

POPPER, K. R., *The Poverty of Historicism*, Boston, Beacon Press, 1957.

PUMPHREY, R. J., *The Origin of Language*, Liverpool, Liverpool University Press, 1951.

RAPHAEL, D. D., "Darwinism and Ethics," *A Century of Darwin*, ed. S. A. Barnett, Cambridge, Harvard University Press, 1958.

RENSCH, B., *Neure Probleme der Abstammungs lehre*, Stuttgart, Enke, 1947.

RENSCH, B., "The Intelligence of Elephants," *Scientific American*, February, 1957.

ROBERTS, M., *The Behavior of Nations*, London, Dent, 1941.

ROE, A., and SIMPSON, G. G., *Evolution and Behavior*, New Haven, Yale University Press, 1958.

ROHEIM, G., *Psycho-analysis and Anthropology*, New York, International Universities Press, 1950.

ROSS, D., *Foundations of Ethics*, New York, Oxford University Press, 1949.

RYLE, G., *The Concept of Mind*, New York, Barnes & Noble, 1950.

SAPIR, E., "The Grammarian and His Language," in *Selected Writings of E. Sapir*, Berkeley, University of California Press, 1951.

SCHROEDINGER, E., *Science and Humanism*, New York, Cambridge University Press, 1951.

SCHROEDINGER, E., *Nature and the Greeks*, New York, Cambridge University Press, 1954.

SCOTT, J. P., "The Analysis of Social Organization in Animals," *Ecology*, **37** (1956), p. 213.

SIMPSON, G. G., *The Meaning of Evolution*, New Haven, Yale University Press, 1950.

SINNOTT, E. W., "The Biological Basis of Democracy," *Yale Review*, 1945.

STEPHEN, K., in *Science and Ethics*, London, Allen and Unwin, 1942, p. 65.

STEWARD, J. H., "Evolutionary Principles and Social Types," *Evolution after Darwin*, **2** (1960), Chicago, University of Chicago Press.

THOMPSON, W. R., "Social Behavior," in Roe, A., and Simpson, G. G., New Haven, Yale University Press, 1958.

THORPE, W. H., *Learning and Instinct in Animals*, Cambridge, Mass., Harvard University Press, 1956.

THORPE, W. H., "The Learning of Song Patterns by Birds," *The Ibis*, **101** (1958), p. 535.

TILLYARD, E. M. W., *The Elizabethan World Picture*, New York, Macmillan Co., 1944.

TINBERGEN, N., *Social Behavior in Animals*, New York, John Wiley & Sons, Inc., 1953.

TINBERGEN, N., *The Herring Gull's World*, New York, Frederick A. Praeger, Inc., 1954.

WADDINGTON, C. H., *The Scientific Attitude*, London, Penguin Books, Ltd., 1941a.

WADDINGTON, C. H., "The Relations Between Science and Ethics," *Nature*, London, **148** (1941b), 220.

WADDINGTON, C. H., *Science and Ethics*, London, Allen and Unwin, 1942.

WADDINGTON, C. H., "Science—Ethics—Religion," *World Review*, July, August, September, 1946.

WADDINGTON, C. H., "Science and Belief," *International Journal of Psychoanalysis*, **28** (1947), 123.

WADDINGTON, C. H., "The Cell Physiology of Early Development," *Recent Developments in Cell Physiology*, New York, Academic Press, Inc., 1954.

WADDINGTON, C. H., *The Strategy of Genes*, London, Allen and Unwin, 1957.

WADDINGTON, C. H., "The Genetic Assimilation of an Adaptive Acquired Character," *Nature*, London, **183** (1959), p. 1654.

WADDINGTON, C. H., "Evolutionary Systems—Animal and Human," *Proceedings of the Royal Institution*, **37** (1959b), 500; also published in *Nature*, London, **183**, 1634 and *Eugenical Review*, **52**, p. 1.

WADDINGTON, C. H., "The Human Evolutionary System," *Proceedings of the Conference on Darwin and Sociology*, 1960.

WADDINGTON, C. H., EWING, A. C., and BROAD, C. D., "Symposium on the Relation Between Science and Ethics," *Proceedings of the Aristotelian Society*, 1943, p. 101.

WATTS, A. W., *The Way of Zen*, New York, New American Library (Mentor), 1959a.

WATTS, A. W., *Beat Zen, Square Zen and Zen*, San Francisco, City Lights Books, 1959b.

WELLS, H. G., HUXLEY, J. S., and WELL, G. P., *The Science of Life*, New York, Doubleday & Co., 1931.

WHITE, L. A., "Ethnological Theory," in *Philosophy for the Future*, New York, Macmillan Co., 1940.

225

WHITE, L. A., "The Individual and the Culture Process," *Centennial Proceedings*, American Association of Advanced Science, Washington, D.C., 1950.

WHITEHEAD, A. N., *An Enquiry Concerning the Principles of Natural Knowledge*, New York, Macmillan Co., 1925.

WHITEHEAD, A. N., *The Concept of Nature*, New York, Macmillan Co., 1920.

WHITEHEAD, A. N., *Symbolism: Its Meaning and Effect*, New York, Macmillan Co., 1927.

WHITEHEAD, A. N., *Modes of Thought*, New York, Macmillan Co., 1938.

WHORF, B. L., "Science and Linguistics," *Readings in Social Psychology*, New York, Henry Holt & Co., 1958.

WITTGENSTEIN, L. V., *Tractatus Logico-Philosophicus*, New York, Harcourt, Brace & Co., 1922.

WITTGENSTEIN, L. V., *Philosophical Investigations*, New York, Macmillan Co., 1953.

YOUNG, J. Z., *Doubt and Certainty in Science*, New York, Oxford University Press, 1951.

INDEX